PRACTICAL N
By Steve H

PRACTICAL MEDITATION

ACKNOWLEDGEMENTS

I would like to thank all my teachers, past, present and doubtless future, for much of the fruits of their hard work are included here as they have become manifest within me. In particular amongst these are Keith and Linda, and Al.

Thanks are also due to all students, past, present and hopefully future for being brave enough to try the meditations you will see in this book. I am also indebted to Margaret Pilling for her help and advice and for ridding me of the effects of hours and hours at the computer writing the book!

Lastly, great love and thanks to the wonderful Amy for typing the manuscript, again.

Contents

Introduction

There are very many books on the subject of Meditation, some good, some not so good, but all with something to offer. The trick is simply to take what feels right for you and discard the rest, maybe for a later day. In my experience as a teacher and practitioner of Meditation there is very little material available that offers the reader techniques that will help them with the business of living daily life. There are thousands (upon thousands) of words written on the theory of meditation and the complexities of spiritual enlightenment. Since I do not make any claims to be able to bestow this upon others or even myself, I do not intend to concern myself with this side of Meditation.

Instead this book will differ in offering you many techniques that you can use and adapt to enable you to better cope with your stress, be generally more relaxed, more aware of yourself and your needs – physical, mental, emotional and spiritual, and overall put yourself in a position to improve the quality of yourself and your life.

In order to achieve this we will take a detailed look at the how, where, when, who and why of meditation to help you understand the subject so as to improve its effectiveness for you. We will explore what happens to you when you meditate, on the different levels of your being. We will discover what can be achieved by its use, where and when best to do it, and indeed how it is best done.

The techniques included in this book are split into sections to which they apply. There are Meditations to achieve and improve relaxation, basic techniques, energy meditations, and meditations for the energy system of the body (these will be explained), meditations for healing – yourself and others – and meditations to aid your development and progression personally and spiritually.

All of the meditations included have been tried, tested and approved by my ever patient students to whom I pay tribute, the ones not approved being consigned to the recycling bin!

I intend this book to be a down to earth book that is approachable to all, not just those already walking a path into the new sunrise of the Aquarian Age. If you have ever wondered what meditation is all about but been too put off by the jargon and the image, settle back and read this book and let it soak in. You will discover that meditation is an easy to acquire habit that can, if you are willing, gently but dramatically change and transform you and your life, making it more meaningful and pleasurable. You will not lose yourself or become ineffectual or weak. Indeed, quite the opposite. You may even find yourself, as I did, campaigning peacefully for projects you believe in, in the forefront of potentially threatening situations. Your meditative awareness will give you the ability to avoid violence however and you will have helped improve the world or at the very least made people think.

This is not to say that meditation is only for those willing to park themselves in front of bulldozers and diggers, for it is one of the few subjects that are truly available to all. Children can meditate once of a certain age, the elderly can meditate, so can students, computer programmers, solicitors, counsellors, administrators, even authors (and their publishers!) as the professions of some of my own students testify. Many large companies are now including regular classes to help their workforce, though these are still referred to as 'stress management' rather than meditation – they're getting there!

This book will also aid those teachers of meditation (and stress management) as it will supply you with a plethora of techniques you can use in your classes. Please feel free to do so. It is my hope that the meditation included here will be used by many people in a spirit of exploration and development. Some no doubt you will not like and some you will. Some you may feel you can improve, in

2

which case do so with vigour and dedication – then write to the publishers to let me know the results. Together we can set out our wares in the market place for inspection and trial by all and in so doing perhaps allow a new awareness to move into some people as they continue their path through this wondrous and amazing world.

This new awareness is moving rapidly through the various peoples of the world in as many different ways as countries. This, we are told, is indicative of the shift into the Aquarian Age, when we need to live by new principles and means. I have found that meditation is the cornerstone to that new awareness, not only in my spiritual life and higher aspirations by guiding me, but in the way that I live my life, the food I eat, the clothes I wear, the people I respect and choose to see, the work that I do and my own view of myself. Meditation you see, is very practical, just as in many esoteric teachings the most spiritual place for us is right in front of our eyes – our much maligned Mother Earth. Meditation does not have to be filled with mystery and wonder, with your inner vision always filled with cloaked and hooded, glowing figures. Meditation is for me and I know thousands of others, the cornerstone of spiritual development, but that development takes place in day to day life as you go about your business of living.

After many years of a (mostly!) daily practice of meditation I can say that it is this that really 'keeps me together' and enables me to remain truly in control of my life and my destiny. Through my meditations I am able to keep aware of the underlying energies and forces, both within and without myself, that shape my life and the reality I experience. From this awareness I am able to make decisions that I know within are the right ones. I am able to apply the wisdom (sometimes) gained in the meditations to help me avoid excesses and actions that are not beneficial for me. In this, meditation is the key to an inner peace and satisfaction that enables me to gaze out of my window to an ancient and beautiful hill and know that all is well with the world, despite wars, famine, rape, murder, addiction and the newly built motorway next to the hill. This may sound foolish or illogical, but these are things that cannot be explained, only experienced.

But this book is not about such mystical statements. My aim is to take the mystery out of meditation and make it understandable and approachable as a natural means by which to better understand yourself and the world you live in. Through a regular meditation practice I can tell you that it is possible to achieve a deep and satisfying balance of the body, mind and spirit. Where this is likely to lead you, only you can discover.

Let this book guide you then through the mystical maze of meditation and arrive at a quiet and green place at the centre of the maze, where others of like mind may follow and you may sit in peace, in solitude if you wish, and let the world run crazy around you, whilst you remain centred and still in the centre of yourself and all things. There are no short cuts through this maze, no easy or quick way, but by earnest and dedicated application, watching and remaining awake and aware of your route and experiences along the way, you will reach that centre. Meditation requires regular practice and patience. Like anything worth having, effort and investment of yourself must be mad first. In time your hours spent sitting with closed eyes thinking you are wasting your time will be more than amply repaid.

Once you have reached the centre of the maze you will know your way out. It will be the same route as you took in but it will look and feel different. The greenery may seem more verdant and alive, as if it flows with life. You too will glow with this life (though you do in fact do this already, you just may not realise this yet!) and so the intrinsic connection between yourself and all things is discovered. This leads you to think, feel and act more responsibly, thus becoming in control of your life and yourself. In the headiness of all, keep your feet on the ground, see where you are going and don't forget to meditate!

Chapter 1 - Take a Deep Breath

Meditation has been used for thousands of years all over the world. There are consequently many different approaches to the subject of Meditation and many people have written and spoken extensively about it. Meditation has thus become filled with many images and opinions, some true, some false. This has tended in recent years to result in a mass of confusion presented to the curious on their first enquiry or experience. How do you know which way is best and who can you trust to teach you properly?

The easy answer to this question, given by many teachers, would be to trust your instinct or intuition. This is all very well, but how do you know what that is and whether you can trust it when you discover it? In one way, meditation needs no teacher other than yourself. Most people are aware that to meditate involves sitting quietly and being relaxed. This alone is ultimately enough and if you do sit long enough in this way, if you have the patience, you would slip into a meditative state.

You would then perhaps expect inner realisations to follow, popping into your head from nowhere, because you are so relaxed and serene. This may happen, but then again, it may not. You may sit there wondering what to have for dinner and how Aunt Mabel is. You may think that this approach will lead you to enlightenment and that this will be the end of all your problems. And you might even be right, in which case please let me know at once what to do!

Meditation has become imbued with a popular image and idea in people's minds. Often trough ridicule, meditation has been portrayed as something practised by monks in Eastern countries or hippies, the inference being that it is only those who are weak, ineffectual, out of touch with reality, or who want to disappear from the world and pretend that everything is beautiful all of the time, that meditate. It is true that hippies do meditate and doubtless monks in Eastern countries too, but as mentioned in my Introduction, so do a great many other folk. Whilst it is true that some of these3 may initially want or expect to be able to use meditation as a method of escapism, others want to get in touch with themselves, weed out their insecurities and failings and progress through life. To these people, with patience and dedication will come the fruits of meditation. To the escapists, whilst locked in the cages of a narrow view, comes escape!

I have had many a student come to me in the past who simply wants to live in a permanent state of Meditation, including one who even proudly reported that she practised while driving – which I do NOT recommend! You just cannot live this way all the time, the current condition of our society and world will not allow it. So when I see a student in this condition I know there is work to be done. They may simply be at a stage in themselves where they need to rest for a while and take time out from the strain of facing the world. That is fine and meditation will allow this on a daily basis, but it is not an escape route from facing up to reality. We must be clear here that life can be approached in a meditative way, balanced and measured, but we cannot be in a state of meditation all of the time.

Many students have seemed to almost float into my meditation room for their introductory session. Those that come into the room full of nerves and declaring that they do not know why they are here are easy – they are ripe and ready to open up from within themselves and discover all there is to know. The 'floaters' think they know it already. Which do you fit into?

Before any real progress can be made with the floaters, it is necessary to stop them floating. How long this takes depends entirely on them. Some students don't stop floating and decide that meditation is either not for them or that they can do it by themselves. Rarely do I find them still meditating when our paths next cross. Of course they have valid reasons: the kids, work, moving house and so on. They are just not yet ready to face the world or themselves. When they are ready they will return and the work can begin.

Let us look a little closer at the floater. They may well have practised meditation before, but never quite found the method that is right for them. They will have attended umpteen courses and workshops but have doubts about many of them. They have answers for any one they meet, and are always eager and willing to declare their problems to the world. Never do they have a negative thought or enact an evil deed or wrong someone. Whilst they may occasionally eat, they most certainly would never drink alcohol – pubs are filled with far too many negative vibrations anyway. They will often be a practitioner of complementary therapy and never have any money (these last two are not necessarily linked!).

I wonder if any of this is sounding familiar. If it is, then be proud and declare that you are a floater – come out and float in public! Perhaps then the ridicule you would be met with would bring you back down to Earth with the requisite bump. It is necessary first for us to see reality for what it is in order to use anything, meditation or otherw2ise, to change and improve it to be more in keeping with our real desires. This means that we must be in a constant state of vigilance to ensure our minds are open and perceive things from different perspectives. Of course we must also know what our real desires are and to do this we must look within and discover what is clouding out view, what is holding us back, how our character and personality may be shaped by our childhood or even previous lifetimes.

Meditation can do all this and much more, but you must be willing and approach of your own free will. If you are reading this, it is quite likely that you are indeed ready, in which case keep reading! But what of our beloved floater? How do we get them to see they are floating in the first place, for they will not be able to see that their feet do not reach the ground? They never look down you see, the clouds being far too appealing. Often they drift, like the clouds and join with other clouds. Meditation groups are often full of floaters and in these nothing ever happens, meditation included. Before any floaters who have recognised themselves in these words throw the book down in disgust at my attitude, let me say that the potential in you is enormous. Simply look down and see the real world for what it is. It is only by accepting the way you really are, warts and all and accepting that the world is a horrible place sometimes that you can begin to see reality. The world can be a beautiful place too sometimes, even most of the time and meditation helps us to realise this. But we cannot see the beauty without seeing the ugliness. It is even possible then to look at ugliness and see beauty within.

If your perception of meditation is such that you will become a floater when you meditate, in my approach you are wrong. In my experience it is the same in other meditation traditions also. Meditation does not welcome floaters; it is far too real and practical for all that. Of course should you come across one of the many groups that are led by a floater, run, while you still can!

Many people when I tell them that I meditate assume that I sit in a room that is filled with incense, my legs wrapped around my neck, chanting. Such is meditation's popular image. As mentioned before, there are many approaches to the subject and this image indeed one of them and a very old and respected one. This Eastern practice embodies and ancient and sacred tradition and it is sad that many see it fit for ridicule, especially without trying it first. I used to be a little embarrassed at telling people that I meditated, but I learnt that the inner strength it have me was such a valuable thing that I saw the ridicule as ridiculous! So now I am proud.

Still however, this image persists. I hope through this book to go some way to promoting a rather different image of the meditator. It is possible to use meditation techniques on the train, waiting for the bus, walking the dog and even eating dinner, as well as sitting in a silent room with candles, incense and so on.

This brings to mind an oft quoted saying of the Buddha: 'Don't meditate, be in Meditation'. The acts of eating, walking and so on can become a meditation so that one's life is lived in a balanced and measured way, avoiding a path of excess. So we live life in a meditative way, accepting what life presents to us and adapting accordingly, from a place within ourselves of peace and understanding of the events we experience.

The meditation techniques given in this book are culled from many different sources and influences and from spiritual and other traditions the world over. Sometimes I have discovered that my conclusions about how we can work with meditation fit nicely into the Zen philosophy or some such. This is pleasing for I am keen to borrow from any tradition. I call the way I work with meditation, Western. This is in the sense that it is not Eastern and to distinguish it from that universally accepted image described above.

There is of course nothing wrong with that image or that approach, it is misleading however for people to think that this is all meditation does and that this is the only way. 'Western' meditation is more suited to Western bodies and minds. It utilises techniques and practises from the West, East and bits in between. It has differences in its posture, its methods and its aims, all of which we shall explore.

One of the differences between Eastern and Western meditation is in noise. It is often assumed that meditation must be done in silence and indeed many meditations are done in silence, at least on the part of the meditator. In the Western approach it is quite common to have one person guiding a group or an individual through a specific meditation, technique or journey. We in the West are taught and molly-coddled through our lives so much that we rarely have to think for ourselves and really stretch our minds and use our brains. Perhaps this is because all the conveniences of Western lifestyle make life easier and simpler for us. At the time of writing many capitalists are rubbing their hands in glee and rushing off to China to exploit – sorry, explore the new market opening up there. What effect the Western invasion will have remains to be seen. In the meantime those in the East continue to live on their wits, each one probably more alive and fulfilled than a hundred Western robots.

As such, through history, those in cultures without our safe and cosy society have needed to use their minds, their memories and instincts to a much greater degree than us. Consequently they adapt much easier to the practice of silent meditation as they are able to focus and concentrate their minds and are more able to recall what they have experienced and felt during the exercise once they have finished. We tend to need a chaperone to lead us safely through ourselves as we once again learn to live in a way closer to the instincts of Nature. To this end, the meditations given in this book could be used in a group setting or by yourself. You will need to read them through many times before attempting them to ensure that you really have memorised the method so that you can follow it through smoothly and without having to stop to think what comes next. To make life easier I have recorded some of the meditations which are available to you in on C.D.

Of course there is nothing to stop you recording your own. If you do this, try not to sound too wooden and don't read from the book like a script. Read the meditation through enough times so that you can memorise it and then record it in your own words. Then listen to it several times so that you are familiar with it and also with the sound of your own voice. You will need to get to the stage that it is irrelevant whose voice it is talking to you. The content of what is said should be all that you hear, in the background to what you are experiencing.

Why?

Before we begin to look at the practicalities of meditation we must first examine our motivation for meditating. It is perhaps necessary to examine your motives in anything of significance you do in life, to remain aware and to give our-self a sense of control. Meditation is no exception to this common sense rule of thumb. Some aspects of this have already been dealt with above, in our examination of floaters and some of the preconceptions held by people concerning meditation. Let us look a little closer at motivation.

We have seen that a desire to escape is misplaced, for meditation makes one more aware of one's self and the effect of life upon the self and the self upon life. This comes from a quiet and still place within and so is subtle in its methods of communication. This occurs mentally but also physically, as we shall see later in the book. It is perhaps this gentle subtlety that causes people to think they can escape from facing and dealing with life. Of course, should this be ones motivation there will be disappointment initially. Should one persevere however, the individual can and will find that inner place that allows them to accept the reality of their life and so begin the process of shaping it to be more in keeping with their wishes and desires.

This is a gradual process and can take many years, even a whole lifetime. This brings us to another motivation, that of time. Meditation takes time to learn its methods and to experience its effects. If then the motivation is to acquire a quick system of happiness, to enable one to continue life in the same way as before, but happier due to a meditation practice, disappointment will surely follow, if not disillusionment, both of the self and with meditation.

The state of happiness for each of us is subjective, it comes and goes. The trick perhaps is to accept this and in so doing embrace the down times as well as the up. There is a popular theory that whatever we experience fully disappears. If we therefore embrace our depression, anxiety, illness or whatever, it will disappear. Of course this can be true of our happiness, or our new romance, baby, house, car or whatever and so we must learn to find a balanced and measured way between these two, following an even line as opposed to one with peaks and troughs.

So meditation will not make you 'happy' nor is it quick. Meditation is one of those subjects which you never stop learning about. |Thus any teacher or author of meditation can only pass on what they have learnt from experience. There is a great emphasis in our society on speed and swift acquisition of goods.

11

Meditation stems from a time and motivation very different. Its benefits are not initially tangible and take time to acquire and realise. Simply, this must be accepted for meditation to 'work' for each person that comes to it.

It is my experience that the goodness that comes out of meditation is not just for ourselves. As a species humanity is essentially a sharing creature, not a selfish one. This statement is obviously one open to great debate and discussion, which I offer for your consideration. The fruits of meditation, which we shall taste shortly, count among their number identity with others, a realisation of our connection with all things, the awareness of our ability to heal (ourselves and others(and a sense of inner peace and contentment. It is my experience and subsequent belief that there is an instinctive desire in the human system that wishes share the sense of peach within once it is gained, with others who we perceive do not have it. This is not evangelistic, but a quiet offering to those that approach, of what we know to be true for us, in the hope of it being true for others in need.

For myself, this means that a higher motivation for meditation is that of service. If one seeks from meditation only selfish goals and ends, then I feel that there is an omission of a deep satisfaction that can result from the sharing of the feeling within of inner peace. This is rather like the difference between solitary and group meditation. This does not come from a self-satisfaction of 'I did this for them' train of thought, but a deeper level of knowing that one has truly helped another to evolve in the right way for them and the ability to share that experience.

Whilst a degree, even large, of motivation for the self is good, such as a desire for inner contentment, acceptance of one's limits, or discovery of one's abilities and potentials, there is perhaps a higher calling that these things can lead on to. They are ultimately not for the self and so neither is meditation. It should be mentioned here that this does not mean we should take responsibility for others and their choice of path through life, whether constructive or destructive. We can offer help, but we cannot rescue.

It is also good to look at whether we really believe meditation can work or not, when we begin. If we persevere it is true that meditation can work for all, but for some another path may seem to be more effective. So does meditation work? All I can say here is that it does for me and I believe it can for you, whoever you are. The process and effect of meditation bypasses logic, as we shall see. This means two things: one, that it is not necessary to mentally believe in meditation for this to work and two, that it is necessary to mentally believe in meditation for it to work!

Since meditation bypasses logic it does not matter what we believe about it. If we allow it to, it will work. However, what is lodged deep in our minds at the subconscious level of belief has a direct effect upon your perception of reality. If you think deep within yourself that meditation is all bosh then your experience of it is likely to be bosh too. If however, you have logical doubts but want it to work, then with time, patience and effort on your part, it will work. Your conscious doubts will be surpassed by your subconscious experience and knowing. In fact the meditation will work anyway; it is just a matter of our realising that it works.

So, consider what you believe about meditation. Are your preconceptions that of the guru, monk or hippy sitting in a room pretending to be a tree but fooling themselves and not facing reality or do you think that there is a deeper reality within that you have not yet discovered and hope that meditation will show it to you? Be aware then as you begin to acquire a meditation practice in your life that your beliefs and preconceptions will rise to greet, challenge, ridicule and finally applaud you.

Having looked at some of the weaknesses within we may have about approaching meditation; let us turn our attention to the positivity of the subject. These will not take the form of a long list of benefits you will acquire from practising meditation, as you will discover these for yourself as you follow the exercise in the book through. Rather we will look at some of the positive motivations that exist in approaching meditation for the first time.

It may be that you wish to gain a certain something inside yourself from meditation that you cannot define but have a vague sense is there anyway. So you stumble along in your meditation practice, not really knowing why you are doing it or where it is going to lead you. This does not necessarily matter, for as we have seen it is not necessary to believe it works for it to work. It is perhaps necessary to believe that you can do it, but that is different. Meditation is not a technique that you must learn or a way of acting; it is an experience, so you can therefore 'do it'. If you believe that through meditation you will find and experience this inner part of yourself, you are far more likely to do just that. If you don't really believe that meditation will show this to you, it will be much harder to find. So the positive thing to do is to consider what you expect from your meditations and what you consciously think it will do for you. Then it is much more likely to happen.

You may want peace of mind from your meditation practice, or perhaps greater awareness of yourself, improved health or simply to be more relaxed. These goals are quite laudable and indeed, achievable. Many times my students have communicated these desires and many times they have been found. These are all quite common goals and perhaps to be expected from meditation. They are certainly not beyond being achieved by anyone, but it is worth being aware of the principle that 'familiarity breeds contempt'. By this, I mean that it is important not to assume that because these are the standard expectations expressed from meditation, they apply to you. One or more or all of those listed may apply to you and indeed be true, but it is important to go through the process of considering why this is the case. It can certainly help to consider for a time what your concept of peace of mind, understanding, better health or relaxation is, to discover which you have and which you do not.

Once this has been realised you then have a firm and clear basis from which to start. You may still not know why you are meditating, other than the hope that it will help, but you will at least have a yardstick to measure your progress against. How can you know when you have become more relaxed if you do not experience how tense you are first? How can you improve your health until you have identified your illness or disease?

Of course these things are not obligatory prior to commencing meditation. They are perhaps preferable, but can very often be realised in the early stages of adopting a regular practice of meditation. You are therefore able to quite successfully and effectively begin to meditate without knowing why, how, when or where but doing it anyway. It will still work, if you have the correct attitude of mind. Put simply this attitude is one of gentleness wit yourself, love of yourself, patience and persistence. Of course all these things can take a long time to acquire in the first place, so beginning meditation with these as your aim is fine too there is enough there to keep you occupied for many a year! Meditation, whichever way it is approached or understood and for whatever reason, is entirely beneficial.

How Often?

Having considered our options and motivations we are now in a position to look at the practicalities of meditation. One of the popular misconceptions about meditation is that it must be practised every day without fail. Whilst it is true to say that a daily session of meditation is one of the best and most effective ways of realising its benefits, it is not essential in order to gain from its use. It really cannot be said often enough that meditation is a subject that will repay you directly in proportion to what you invest, the investments necessary here being time, emotion, concentration and effort. We all have these things in abundance if we have a care to look. What we need to do, we make time to do.

The progress you make with your meditation practice is then entirely at your own pace and depth. If you are lucky enough to have a teacher to guide you, there should be no pressure to meditate other than when you are in the class, but there should be all the encouragement you need. Many people are put off by the thought of having to add into their daily tasks a time of meditation, on top of feeding the children, making the breakfast, dealing with the post and the other thousand things we invent to keep us occupied.

It is far better to simply adopt a meditation practice when you are ready to and build on this gradually and gently, when you want to. In this way your bodily system and your mind will adjust easily and naturally to the new messages your meditation will be giving it. Of course you must have a certain amount of discipline with yourself to ensure you actually do your meditations, but more of this later. For now, we cans imply introduce a meditation at a level we are each comfortable with as an individual.

I would say here that a daily practice is the optimum for the benefits of meditation to occur fully and I always encourage my students to achieve this in time. This is in part because our perspective on our internal and external lives can change overnight as the subconscious mind, active during the night rather than our everyday conscious mind, is allowed to communicate its messages to the brain. We thus wake up with a new feeling or thought. By meditating, we can access that new thought or feeling fully, assimilating it and making a better informed decision as to its relevance. We can also descend directly into the subconscious through meditation and realise its information there.

It is common to find that the daily practice of meditation, once it is acquired, becomes part of one's life. It is not a hobby or even a habit, but becomes part of what and who one is. It becomes necessary in order to remain fully alert and stable within oneself. It is not however addictive in any way, other than something you want to do. Life however has its own habit that of causing changes to occur, often unexpectedly. When this happens we are often unable to keep our appointed slot with our meditative selves. When this happens it is important not to feel guilty or bad. Do not resent the intrusion into your habit but accept it and deal with it, then when you can, come back to your meditation.

Feeling guilty will not do you any good at all and you do not have a duty to perform your meditation daily. It is important however to realise that we are creatures of habit. Meditation can become a habit, pleasurable and helpful, but still a habit. It is important to distinguish here between the daily performances of your meditation, as opposed to the experience. This is why effort is required, constantly. Meditation is not something that you just do each day without considering it. It is a kind of active passivity.

The habit of meditation needs then to be disciplined in order to avoid losing it. Once it is part of your routine, whether daily, weekly or otherwise, it is best to remain regular in its execution. If you experience a break in that routine, whether forced or not, you will need to ensure that the break does not become permanent. This will in large part be avoided naturally once you have consciously realised and come to value what meditation does for you but in the meantime, and also as a permanent state, vigilance must be exercised to ensure the habit does not slip into oblivion. I find that if I miss meditation for longer than two days, I can feel the lack of the effects within me. This may be mentally, emotionally, physically, and spiritually or all four, dependent on what is happening in my life at the time.

In this way the natural benefits of meditation make themselves clear by their absence. This I use as my warning light and I make sure I have a good meditation session as soon as practical. This is not obsessive, only valuing and taking care of myself. When you have breaks then, do not feel guilty, accept the situation, deal with it as best you are able and come back to meditation. The habit stays as part of your system and you are the better for it. The effects and in some ways the experience of meditation is and are for the most part, subtle. Do not expect to feel that all has changed and is now wonderful in your life after one week's meditating. This subtlety is one of the main reasons too for guarding against loss of habit.

The inner awareness that comes from meditation is a subtle one as in general are the realisations that emerge from our subconscious during it. These filter into our minds and bodies over a period of time and we thus adopt a more serene and understanding posture in life. This stays with us, hovering as if just below our conscious everyday awareness.

It is so easy, especially in the speed of overdose of activity and information in our society today, to lose the vigilance we need to monitor that awareness. It is so easy to tell yourself you do not have the time to meditate or have too much to do. Thus we become less and less aware of the benefit we gain when we 'forget' to meditate for a prolonged period of time. We then forget that subtlety itself and the habit is broken, the awareness gone from our conscious minds. We then believe either that meditation does not work or that we are too busy and that other things have to take precedence. We shall see later in the book that we can gain more time for ourselves if we include meditation I our lives and that we can do those things that are so important so much the better if we meditate.

So how often you mediate is an individual choice and will adapt and change to your living circumstances as they change. You should not force yourself to meditate and I will say one last time, not to feel guilty if you do not.   Never though, underestimate its value. Remember it is a subtle inner process, not instantly tangible. You cannot demonstrate its benefit to you other than by being yourself, aided and abetted by your meditative awareness in everything you do. In this way you are 'in meditation', not meditating, so Buddha will be pleased with you.

When?

Having dealt with the 'how often' of meditation we will move on to the when. This will in part be determine3d by your living circumstances. For those who work shifts it will of course be more difficult to impose a regular time of meditation. For those with small) or adult!) Children to care for meditation will be easier when the children are not there or are asleep. There are many other such obstacles we face in deciding when best to meditate.

As has already been mentioned, a regular time is perhaps best and more conducive to obtaining the best from your meditation sessions. When this is, will depend you yourself, apart from living circumstances. Some people are almost nocturnal, feeling that they come alive more through the night, no matter when they work. For these people meditation at the beginning of this period may perhaps be best. For those of us who are creatures of the daytime, we may well find that a while after rising is our best time for meditation. There is an element of trial and error her for each person.

I have found that a regular time, without being obsessive about which minute, works better. As stated before we are creatures of habit. Mentally you will become conditioned to the time that you do your meditation and your conscious mind will more happily give up its control as it will know what is happening and that it is not about to be extinguished forever.

Physically your own internal and constant body clock will know and expect to meditate around the time you usually do, once it has become used to doing it. This is also partly why we can feel and be aware of those effects and benefits not happening in the times when we break from our meditation.

Personally my morning routine makes provision for my meditation. This is before eating breakfast, but after having been 'up' for an hour or so. This ensures that I am not carrying the dregs of my sleep with me, yet it is early enough so that I have not begun to consider the business of the day. This seems the best time for me and I would certainly recommend this to those with a regular routine of the '9 to 5'. Others have found that the lunch break provides the perfect opportunity for meditation.

The importance of food and digestion should be mentioned before we go any further. Food makes us feel heavy when it is still in our stomachs and so trying to slip into a light state of meditation and letting the physical body relax when it is trying to work gives us conflicting messages. Concentration becomes difficult as a consequence and this is one of the corner stones to many meditations. Equally, and empty stomach can be just as distracting, for you will be tempting yourself to have visions of food drifting through your mind when you should be meditating! If you meditate in the morning your stomach will soon become used to accepting food and a little while after you have woken up.

Whilst on this subject it should also be mentioned that meditation wile alcohol is in the blood is not recommended. I would refuse admission to any person attending my groups smelling of alcohol. It is ultimately best to avoid alcohol for at least 12 hours prior to meditating. Alcohol dulls the system and makes you less responsive. You are thus making your meditation much harder work for yourself than need be and you cannot guarantee that the results are the product of a mind with a clear view of reality. The same is true for drugs, legal and illegal, though of course many people have tried experimenting with various substances to enhance the experience. I will leave this to you!

The danger of falling asleep is one that needs to be given a little attention in deciding when during the day to meditate. Many people think that last thing at night, prior to retiring, is the best time to meditate as they are more relaxed then. The danger however is that sleep will simply take over. Whilst it is true to say to a degree that the body obviously needs to rest and if meditation induces this, it is a good thing, it is not the optimum response one would like or can get from meditation. The mind and body will be expecting sleep and rest at the kind of time it is used to, not meditation.

Physically the responses given to these unconscious messages from the mind promote its slower and duller working. In meditation the mind is best relaxed yet alert, aware and responsive. Once the habit of falling asleep during meditation is acquired, it becomes difficult to get out of, as it is very nice to do. Falling asleep after a relaxation or meditation session does provide for a good and deep sleep for those times when this is difficult I have included a technique in Chapter 6.

There are other theories that say that the afternoon is the best time to meditate as the 'energy' is more conducive at that time. The path of the Sun reaches its height, in heat, power and effect when it is highest I the sky above us. When this is will depend where you live of course, but once this zenith has been reached the Sun's effect upon us is not to stimulate and increase, as it is during the morning. The Sun, being the source of life without which we cannot live, calms its force after noon and so this is perhaps why this time is more conducive to meditation. The energy we receive from the Sun is more in keeping with that which we wish to achieve in our meditation. Of course one could apply this same argument to dusk, for once the Sun has set a magical time ensues as we cross from day to night and many people find that they are more sensitive then. There are many theories and opinions as to when the best time to meditate is, as you can see. Trial and error and your own feelings are the only real guide as to when is best for you.

What to Wear?

When you are performing your meditation you also need to give some consideration to your clothing. This is not for the sake of appearance, but for comfort. It is vital that you and your body feel comfortable to enable you to both physically and mentally relax fully. If you are wearing clothes that restrict your movement, or ability to let go of your muscles, then you will not be able to relax to the degree that is really necessary to be in a state of meditation.

One example of this is trying to meditate whilst in shirt and tie as this causes restriction around the neck, however good the cut of the shirt. This is easily remedied of course by loosening your tie and undoing the top button of your shirt! If this is your usual work wear or something similar there is also a psychological effect to be considered. Should your meditation time be in a break from work during the day, which is fine in itself, you will need to consciously tell yourself that you do not have to put on the persona of your working self and personality for the time of your meditation. You would find otherwise that the content and responses you perceive in your meditation would be coloured by the responsible, working part of yourself. You may perceive a need for play and freedom in your meditation but this could be easily repressed by your responsible self, acting in accordance with the mentality you adopt whilst working, just as you should. So take time to tell yourself that you can let go of your working persona and attitude and just be your true self. Of course discovering what your true self is, is enough meditation fuel for many a good and productive session!

For those that perform their meditation out of the working environment there is a greater flexibility available in clothing that can be mad use of. The obvious requirement here is to avoid tight jeans or tight clothes of any sort, as explained above. Loose fitting but comfortable clothes are the best, that you feel comfortable in both mentally and physically. It is also important to ensure that you are warm enough. Slowing the body's heart rate and brain wave down, which often occurs during meditation, has a tendency to reduce the temperature of the body and you will become more sensitive to any slight chill or draught that might exist around you.

It is for this reason that many people cover themselves with a blanket or sheet to perform their meditation each day. Aside from ensuring warmth, this has the added benefit of giving a womb like feel, being safe, and nurturing. This is of great use in meditation as the more 'safe' one feels the more likely one is to be able to let yourself feel things deeply and truly. This has great benefits in healing meditations and for the general pleasure of the meditative experience. Some may however feel that a blanket of covering is restricting or smothering and so, as with all things in meditation, you must discover what is right for you, which may not be right for any other.

Another option is to keep a special set of clothes or perhaps a robe for meditation. Over a period of time this will accrue a special 'feel' to it, as it becomes cloaked (no pun intended here!) with the energy of life force you transmit during your meditations. This will help the effectiveness and clarity of what you experience. There is also a psychological effect of a special robe or clothing. This will occur each and every time you put the clothing on, without your thinking each and every time you put the clothing on, without your thinking of it or doing anything else. Your subconscious mind will soon know that when your eyes see the clothes and your body feels them, that it is time for meditation. It will thus be ready and willing, which it will not always be, to allow you to relax deeply and access information from its murky depths.

The same can be done with a special blanket or even holding in your hand or pocket a particular piece of cloth or handkerchief that you associate with meditation, for whatever reason. This goes beyond the childlike habit of the security blanket, though this can help, and will have the same psychological effect as wearing the clothes themselves. Should you acquire this helpful habit do be aware of what you do with your robe or cloth between meditations. It should not be left lying about for others to handle or to acquire a residue of every day effects, whether positive or not, as this will remove the light in which you view it and take away its special, reserved feel for you when you try to use it. It is a good idea to buy a special cloth that is only ever used for this purpose and is then placed in its own bag or in the wardrobe etc. Again you must make your own choices and decisions here but do remember that all these things are not necessary or vital for you to meditate effectively but they may help and you may derive some use and pleasure from them.

One last point to mention on the subject of clothing concerns footwear. It is usually best to remove any footwear, however comfortable it may feel, as there is always an element of restriction about the feet, which will prevent proper relaxation. This is an important part of the process of going into meditation as we shall see. By not allowing the muscles in the feet to relax fully, you are preventing the flow of life force energy down, which when we come to exploring the essential meditation technique of grounding and connecting, we will see is vital. So, wherever you are, take your shoes off.

Where?

Another subject that needs to be given some consideration is that of where to perform your meditation. Once more there are physical and psychological effects that will ensue from your choice of place. This will in part be determined by whether you choose to sit or lie down to perform your meditation and your choice here will obviously have an effect on the location of your meditation. It is perfectly acceptable to be lying down to meditate and we will see as we progress that some techniques are better done this way. Some are better performed sitting and we will discuss exact posture shortly.

If you choose to lie down to meditate you will need to consider where this will be. Should you decide that the bed is the place for you, then you must be extremely careful that you do not fall asleep. I would have to say that tempting though this may be, it is not advisable to meditate whilst lying on one's bed. If lying down, the floor is a good a place as any, perhaps with a blanket beneath you just to give you a little softness. In fact the hardness of the floor can be of benefit in meditation. As you relax your body when going into a meditative state, you can allow the solidity and firmness of the floor to support your body, knowing the security of this in your mind. This alone can be a meditation, letting yourself become completely weightless and letting the floor really support you. You could then go on to feeling yourself sinking into the floor and seeing what you find down there. When you finish, come back up to the surface.

Places and rooms do acquire their own atmosphere and feeling, dependent on what happens in them, both over a prolonged period of time. Rarely would one choose to meditate in the kitchen for instance, it would just not seem or feel right. This is because this place is one of production and activity and the atmosphere here reflects this. It is not a place for quiet reflection and stillness. Neither is the bedroom ideal, for this is a place to sleep and rest. This is not the only reason for meditation, as we shall see, and psychologically the effect of trying to relax for meditation in the bedroom will tell the brain that it is time to switch off and sleep for a while. In meditation the ideal state is a relaxed body, free of tension and activity and a mind that is relaxed also, yet alert and responsive at a deep level. You cannot be this way if you are asleep!

It is of great benefit to have a permanent place that is your meditation space, or perhaps your meditation chair. This will acquire its own little atmosphere that will help you switch in to your meditative self and awareness each time you come to meditate. You can then add a favourite picture that expresses your meditation to you, or perhaps a statue, stone or object from nature, that you like. You may like to light a candle each time you commence your meditation, as I do. This symbolises to me the quiet and stillness of this time, the natural light of the flame creating a beautiful look and feel if it is dark. To me it also signifies the presence of the Spirit, both within me and without, that I feel I become closer to and aware of during meditation. It is a good psychological signal to the brain too that it is meditation time.

The obvious alternative to lying down is to be sitting in a chair, but the choice of chair is also important. The best kind of chair for productive meditation, in the Western tradition and style, is an old fashioned dining room chair, with a tall and straight back, that allows for you to sit straight with your feet firmly on the floor, so as to let the chair take your weight, not your legs or feet. For those more modern souls, there are some chairs available now that are of the folding type that allow for a similar position as that described above.

Those who are perhaps more used to it, may find that sitting on a cushion with legs crossed is the best place for you. Being down on the Earth may feel good for you and the softness of the cushion may feel cosy. This is fine, but do ensure that you are really able to physically relax this way.

You may have a particular place in your home that is your favourite spot to sit in and relax, whether by a window beside your garden or balcony, beneath your favourite picture, beside the fire or whatever. This may allow for that position to easily become your meditation spot and you will be able to make good use of the awareness and feeling of comfort and relaxation that will already exists when you are there. You may wish to experiment with different places and I recommend this until you find a comfortable place that seems to work. Once this has been done, stick with it. You might try meditation outdoors too, perhaps leaning against a tree trunk (do be polite and ask the tree first and thank it afterwards). It can be quite a different experience and a wonderful one to meditate in the open air, perhaps as the Sun sets, and to see the difference in colours from when you close your eyes to when you open them. Do remember that if you try to meditate outdoors that the Earth is often not as comfortable as your cushioned chair, and take something soft to sit on if you think you will need it.

Those who are in the most fortunate position will be able to devote a whole room to relaxation and meditation and perhaps other therapies as well. This will soon feel very different to the rest of your home, acquiring its own special atmosphere and 'energy'. It is good then to adorn the room with natural objects and pictures that you feel express what you gain for your meditation. In this room you can feel safe and secure and free to be you as you truly are, without fear of others seeing or ever knowing, should you not wish them to. This is of immense benefit in accessing the very deepest levels of your inner being to help you on your path through life.

Many of the situations and places described are ideals and certainly not available to everyone who would like to meditate. It is perfectly acceptable to meditate wherever you wish, so long as you are comfortable and can relax. Please view all of the above as suggestions and ideas only, to help you get the best from your meditation, but do not despair in any way if you are not able to select from any of them. Simply adapt to your own circumstances and decide where, when and how is best for you.

Posture

We will now consider the much discussed subject of posture for meditation, before we look at the actual techniques themselves, in the next Chapter. This is a subject that causes great consternation amongst meditation practitioners and teachers but for meditation to be effective you need only find a position that you are able to fully relax your body in and whatever this is, will work for you. It may not for any other person however, as meditation is an individual art. So once again, please view what is offered below as only that – offers that may help you find what is best for you.

When we consider the subject of posture the traditional image of meditation returns to haunt us. Most people assume that you must be in the lotus position, as it is known, sitting with your legs crossed, and feet up on your thighs, fingers touching your thumbs and hands resting on your knees. This is an ancient meditation posture that works wonderfully well, but only for those who are able to sit that way for any length of time, without getting cramp in their legs, a stiff back or neck or cutting off the circulation to their feet. One needs to be trained how to do this properly in order for it to be viable in meditation. The numbers of those who are so

27

trained in the West are relatively few compared to the numbers that actually mediate.

Those of us in the West for the most part grow up sitting in chairs rather than on the floor and so our bodies are not used to sitting in such postures as the lotus position. Consequently, when we try to do this, we find that there is great strain on our knees as the muscles are pulled while we force our feet into position. Unless you are a practitioner of yoga or another similar discipline you are therefore likely to find that trying to sit in this way will not work for you. By all means try, but certainly do not feel that this is the only way and must be mastered. There is a particular method of adopting this posture that you will need to be shown if you are to use it. Since I do not use the Eastern techniques from which this posture comes, I do not make use of it myself.

The standard position for Western meditation that has become widely accepted now is that of sitting relatively upright in a straight backed chair. I have found that this is certainly conducive to a good depth of meditation and suitable for the techniques used in the Western approach to meditation. Your feet should be resting on the floor so you need to make sure that your chair is the correct height to allow you to do this. Your hands should be resting either on your lap or preferably along the tops of your legs. It is best for the palm to face downward for the majority of techniques. This prevents the unwanted outflowing of your own life force or energy that is often stimulated during this type of meditation. There are small centres of this energy in the palm of the hand that will often open during meditation, allowing for the energy to flow out through them. If the hands are faced down, this is less likely to happen if it does; the energy will go back into your legs! Should you be following a meditation to aid healing of another, it is better to reverse the position of the hands and this will be clearly indicated where necessary in this book

Since in meditation we are often concerned with the movement, direction and flow of the life force energy, we must ensure that there is the optimum opportunity for this to occur during our daily practice. The mouth is one area where there is a break in the natural flow around the body of this energy. To overcome this it is good to place the tongue so that it rest on the top of your mouth. You will also find that this will mean that you do not have to swallow at intervals from the build-up of saliva in your mouth, which can be distracting. In this way the tongue creates a bridge for the energy to move across your mouth, thus completing the necessary link around your body. There is a natural instinct to do this anyway and you will find this comfortable.

Try to find a position of sitting wherein you are at a centre of balance, prior to going into your meditative state. This can be found by leaning slightly to each side and back and forwards to find where feels the most comfortable and balanced position for you. This will need to be done each time you sit, but takes only a moment. This will in the main prevent the annoying and potentially dangerous occurrence of your head lolling about while you are in your meditation.

If you become drowsy or are tired before meditating, you may find that the muscles in your neck relax so much that they cannot adequately support your head and so unless it is perfectly balanced it will tip. Your nerves will automatically react to this and snap your head back into place, possibly after you have banged your head on the wall or tree behind you! This is the reason for having a good high back to a straight chair as your head is then supported in the necessary upright position. If this type of chair is not available to you, then the balancing exercise above will suffice. If you are tired this may still be difficult to stop, in which case, sleep, do not meditate, for this is what you need.

Whist in the area of the head let us turn our attention to the eyes. Most people assume that closing one's eyes whilst meditating is necessary and for the most part they are quite correct. However some people find this is not a relaxed position to be in while they are concentrating and prefer to have their eyelids slightly open, lowered and looking downwards. This works well so long as you are not focussed on what your eyes see and do not register the impression in your mind, as this will need to be free to do other things. If you close your eyes do not focus either for you will find the unfocused position much easier and more relaxing for your face muscles. You do not need to try to do anything while meditating, including looking to see more detail of your inner vision. Relax and let things come to you as they surely will. Keep your eyes resting as if they were looking ahead of you, but at nothing.

One last area of the face to give attention to is your expression. The most relaxed and natural position for the face to be in is a slight smile, after the style of the Mona Lisa. This is a natural and easy position for the muscles of the face to be in and prevents you from frowning whilst in meditation, something you may not immediately understand the relevance of. It takes fewer muscles to smile than it does to frown, so make life easier for yourself! Once the pleasant sensation of being in meditation takes over, you may feel like smiling anyway, and might even discover what the Mona Lisa was smiling at!

It is preferable also to have a straight back while meditating. The problem to avoid here is that of thinking that you must remain so rigid that you become taut and tense and never really relax. It is for this reason that I do not place too much emphasis on my students adopting the 'correct' posture. Your back is best kept straight so as to again allow the optimum flow of life force energy around the body. Much mention has already been made of the term 'energy' and will continue to be so used throughout the book. Its exact definition and meaning will soon be made clear, when it is necessary. So, keep a straight back, but do not become overly concerned with this. Again you will find that once you have established the centre of balance in your position this will be much easier and more natural for you.

Lastly as concerns posture, some 'don'ts', to add to the list of 'dos' above. Folding your arms is to be avoided for this will interrupt the flow of that same energy and is also an aggressive gesture, not conducive to meditation. Crossing ones legs (unless in the lotus position or similar) also has a tendency to short circuit your energy flow and will soon become uncomfortable for you.

Distractions

Whilst dealing with the physical body in relation to meditation we should also mention some common distractions, such as coughing and itching. This involves some workings of the conscious mind when we try to get into a meditative state. When we do this we are not using our conscious mind, which day in and day out, controls our thoughts and consequent actions. When we tell it we do not need it for a while, it often panics because it thinks it is going to be forgotten about and will lose control. As we begin to relax then and let go of our conscious control, focussing only on our breath and letting our thoughts go, we suddenly get an urge to cough or scratch somewhere.

This is often because the conscious mind has invented a tickle or an itch or whatever, to remind us that we do need it after all. The best thing to do in this situation is simply to cough, scratch, sneeze or whatever and then come back to your meditation. It serves no purpose to sit there trying not to cough or scratch, other than to make you more tense than when you started. Your conscious mind will soon get used to the idea and accept that its survival is not threatened and the itches will become less frequent and finally disappear. You can then get on with the business of meditation.

Your conscious mind will probably try other tricks to prevent its getting lost or forgotten while you bypass it and meditate. It is because of the fear we have in our mid that we will lose control when we go into meditation that we often find thoughts so distracting. It is as if the conscious mind is reminding us that we haven't yet decided what to have for dinner, what to wear to work that day, that the film we want to see starts at 9pm, that we must tell Fred about the game last night and so on.

When you receive these distractions, as you surely will when you meditate, the best policy to take is simply to acknowledge what you have been doing instead of focussing on your meditation and bring your concentration back. You will need to ensure that you do not feel bad or guilty when you catch yourself doing this and do be aware that everyone does it to some degree or another. Your mind will get used to being quiet, but this takes patience and time. Persevere and your reward will come. You will still find the occasional thought coming into your mind when you are in the middle of a wonderful vision of sweeping beaches, golden sand and warm sunshine. Recognise that you have left the subject of your focus and do not hold onto any thoughts at all. When you begin to do your meditation each time, the knack is to let go of your thoughts as they come so they are not resident in your mind. They are simply passing through, coming and going without really touching you.

In this way you remove any attachment you have with your thoughts and your conscious mind and you can look deeper into yourself. It is at this deeper level that our true thoughts and feelings can be easier accessed and assessed. By using the rather Zen technique of detaching ourselves from our thoughts and our feelings too, we can realise who we are on a deeper level within and so gain a greater awareness and deeper response from it.

There is one other common distraction to meditation that we must give attention to before we begin that of noise. It is extremely rare to find a place in our modern society that is quiet. You may think that if you lived in the country all would be quiet, but there is probably more noise here than anywhere, as the sounds of nature are all around you. It is true that these may be more pleasant than car doors slamming and emergency vehicles sirens, but a bird squawking seemingly right next to your ear just as you slip into a much needed deep state of relaxation is distraction enough.

Silence is often distracting of itself too many people. Once they have managed to find a few minutes of silence in their day to relax, they then find that the silence creates a deafening sound of its own, which serves only to leave them hearing the million and one things buzzing round their head. So do not assume that you must have complete silence in order to meditate. The quietest of houses in the quietest of villages still has noises, whether it be floorboards or walls creaking, taps dripping, electrical appliances buzzing or simply the wind or rain outside. Of course those of us in the centre of a large town or city must add to this list, car doors and engines shouting from people on the street, music from next door and so on. All these serve to make silence a difficult thing to come by.

The very nature of those distracting noises can be annoying if you are trying to meditate or relax. Such noises are very jarring to the ear once identified and it is very difficult, even for the advanced meditator, to just ignore them. One way is to mask the noises around you by playing music softly. This takes away the unspoken awareness that you are meant to be silent now and gives the ear something pleasant to focus on without intruding on your meditative concentration.

Another method of dealing with distracting noise is to use the technique of identifying noise for what it is and then getting on with the meditation, much like the method used for itches and so on. By momentarily recognising that what you hear is a car, a child, music etc. then you can forget about it. Once again we meet the principle that whatever you experience disappears. So just acknowledge that you can hear a noise, identify it if you can or want to, and then move on. There is now no longer any need for your mind to identify the noise as being there at all. You will also find that using this method will serve to make you more aware of your surroundings and what is happening within them and more responsive too. You may also find that your sensitivity to sudden disturbance or loud noise is increased, but remember that you will also be more relaxed as a person due to your meditation, so it may not bother you as much as you may think!

We must now return to the subject of music that we made brief mention to earlier. The choice of music is an important one and obviously an individual preference. One would clearly not choose loud or fast music, whether classical or rock. There is a great deal of music available now that purports to be meditation or relaxation music. Much of this may be relaxing to listen to and very pleasant, but this does not necessarily make it suitable for meditating with, or even relaxing properly.

Ideally your meditation music if you use it should be continuous, with no breaks for new tracks to begin. There should be no sudden noises, from crashing cymbals or drums etc. that could make you jump or start. The music should have a slow pace and you need to feel that it has a calming and peaceful effect upon you that does not make you emotional. If you respond too much emotionally to the music, in the sense of being moved, you will find that your experiences during that meditation will all be coloured by the emotions you are experiencing induced by the music.

You will also need to ensure that your music will last long enough so that you can enter fully into meditation without having to think at all about the music finishing. Many cassette decks these days have automatic systems that cause the machine to switch itself off when a tape finishes. They usually do this with a loud click. When you are deeply relaxed it is surprising how distracting such noises can be and a start like this during meditation is quite unpleasant.

Whilst on this subject it is perhaps sensible to mention that someone shaking you to bring you out of your meditation is not to be advised. If you have children do ensure that they are unlikely to jump on you or shake you whilst you are meditating. Equally if you have animals about ensure that they cannot do the same. Such a severe start or shock as this can in fact be dangerous. If you recall the feeling you have when you are woken suddenly by a loud noise close by and magnify this many times, this will give you the experience of such an occurrence during meditation. This causes the heart to jump wildly and if you are meditating for relaxation this is not the effect you want! On a very serious note, should you be so advanced in meditation as to be able to leave your body, consciously or otherwise, such a shock as that above would cause you to come back to your body with a thump, which at best may cause bruising and at worst a fatal heart attack.

If therefore you live in a shared house or similar, do make sure that the other occupants know you are not to be disturbed while you are meditating. You can easily put up a sign saying 'Do not Disturb' if you don't want them to know what you are doing, or tell them you are sleeping.

The telephone is another obvious distraction that must be dealt with. The simple thing to do is to take it off the hook – problem solved! If you need to remain available then an answering machine is the answer. If so, make sure that you can turn the machine down so that you cannot hear it ring or click. If you know someone has called you, you are likely to want to know who and why and could easily spend the rest of your meditation wondering about this. If someone needs you, they will soon call back and it may do them and you good not to be available all the time anyway!

Aids to Meditation

Having looked at some of the distractions and hindrances to successful meditation, let us now look at how we can help ourselves and examine some of the aids to meditation. Whilst it is true that much of what is given below can be looked upon as meditation paraphernalia and unnecessary, it can also be of use. Look upon these aids then as just that and not vital for you to be able to meditate successfully. If something may help however and is not harmful, why not use it?

You will need to consider lighting when you are meditating inside, as this can have a pronounced effect on your ability to relax as well as inner perception.   Dimmer switches may well have been invented with meditators in mind for they allow the level of light to be adjusted to precisely how you would like it. Some people will find that absolute dark is unpleasant and even threatening and so like a little light, whilst others find that only the dimmest of light is acceptable. The dimmer switch caters for all tastes perfectly.

You can also experiment with lamps and different coloured light bulbs and of different wattage, to give you just the level and shade of light that you like. A soft light is much more conducive to allowing your eyes to relax, even with your eyes closed. Consider sunlight too, as this is particularly bright, maybe more so without parts of the ozone layer, so do not sit facing this. If you do this, you are letting yourself in for an unpleasant awakening when you open your eyes after the meditation too.

Perhaps the most effective and pleasant form of lighting for meditation is candlelight, as we have mentioned previously. There is really no substitute for naked, loving flame and the atmosphere this creates. You can easily vary the level of lighting by adding or subtracting the number of candles you use, but you will find that in the average room just one candle is usually adequate. You might like to keep a candle only to be lit during your meditation, which will add to it being a special time for you.

Do please make sure that your candle will not be knocked during your meditation, by child or animal or you could receive an unwanted baptism of fire! Ensure also that the candle is away from draughts or curtains, or anything flammable. It is best to have a fire blanket or extinguisher handy if you are using candles regularly and know how to put fires out yourself. The rule with candles is that you cannot be too careful.

Smell is a very powerful sense that we respond to at an instinctive level, which still applies during meditation. If you have cooking smells wafting from your kitchen whilst you are meditating it is likely you will think only of how hungry you are during your allotted time. Equally car fumes may drift into your room or cigarette smoke, so it is good to have something to mask these unwanted odours. Incense or essential oil is the answer here and you can utilise their effects to help you.

As you burn either essential oil or incense the smell causes reactions in your brain which release various hormonal fluids in your body which have a physical effect on your system and how you feel etc. It is therefore best to choose an oil or incense that will have a relaxing and expanding effect on your body and mind respectively. Frankincense is the fragrance par excellence here. It is available as an oil or incense and has a powerful smell that will do the required job most effectively. It is this fragrance that will be familiar to many churchgoers from the swinging thurible of incense used there, for precisely the same reason above.

Smell is an individual thing of course and you will need to experiment with other fragrances as well as quantities to find what is right for you. My only recommendation is to ensure that either the oil or the incense you use is pure and from a respected source. Avoid any synthetic blends or makes as these will not contain the properties the pure ones do, and so your brain will not respond and release the chemicals in your body.

You can of course use particular fragrances to help the particular meditation technique you are using. For instance if using the Sleep Meditation given in the book, Lavender will be an excellent aid, as it is excellent for helping us get to sleep. If following a journey through a forest for example, you might like to have the smell of pine about you, as you imagine yourself walking through the sun's rays, streaking through the tall pines that line your path.

You can go the whole way and obtain recordings that are the sounds of a forest, or waves on the shore etc. These may help but do make sure that you are keeping in mind the reality of what you are experiencing. Meditation journeys like this are not an exercise in escaping and what you experience is real, more real in fact than what you can see before you.

After Meditation

When you have completed your meditation there are some considerations that you must give attention to for safety and maximum benefit of what you have done and we will look at these now.

It is common and quite normal to feel a little light headed, or groggy, depending on the technique you have used, when you come out of your meditative state. Further mention of this is made in the grounding and connecting technique given in Chapter 3. For this reason, do not stand up immediately after you open your eyes. You are liable to find yourself back on the floor again very quickly! Give yourself time to adjust your senses, all six of them, to being back in your room or wherever you are. Look around at the walls and your own body. Take time to breathe normally again and take a deep breath or two before you move. Then when you are ready, stand up slowly and make sure that you are steady on your feet before you move.

It is a good idea to have a small snack or drink when you have completed your meditation. This serves to bring your attention back to your body and to the real, tangible world about you. The act of making your body digest food or fluid is good in making this impression clear to both mind and body. It will slow your responses down, which may have accelerated whilst meditating. There is a danger that the light-headedness we can experience in meditation becomes the reason for doing it and then we wish to remain in this state permanently. Another floater is born!

Observing these practices when you begin may seem unnecessary as it may feel to you as if nothing is happening, so it is not necessary to go through this palaver each time you meditate. But we are creatures of habit and so getting into good habits now will avoid you getting into bad ones later, which are much harder to break. This is why all this information is given at the start of the book. These are also good safety measures, for once you have become able to enter a deep state of meditation, which the techniques in this book will enable you to do, it is more important that you know how to come fully out of that state and back to the everyday world, where the fruits of your meditation are intended to apply. In this way, your meditation becomes, as it should be, a journey through a door in your consciousness or awareness, which you open upon entering and close upon leaving.

For precisely this reason it is a good idea to have a notebook in which you record your meditation experiences. This may seem like a chore but it has many benefits. It will again, some become a habit of which you think nothing of doing each time you meditate.

It is best to have the pad handy beside you so that you can record your few lines at most, soon after returning from meditation. Meditation experiences can be like dreams in this respect and indeed conscious dreaming is an apt description of many meditations. This is because what we experience happens at a deeper level in our minds and awareness than the everyday conscious level. As we return we may think then, whilst halfway between being in meditation and everyday consciousness, that we will remember everything without effort. But once you have opened your eyes and come fully back to your room and body you are likely to find that you cannot recall some small detail that meant so much in the meditation. So, just as with dreams it is a good idea to keep a notepad by the bed, write your meditation experiences down as soon after the event as you can.

This does not need to be an essay for each meditation. At most it should be only a few lines or a couple of sentences. State what meditation you did, if anything specific, when, what it felt like and what you feel you got out of it. This way you have a concise diary of your meditations that are an excellent way of charting your progress. Remember that the effects of meditation are subtle and gradual in general so you are unlikely to notice much yourself. If you can look back over your notes it may bring things into perspective for you which you could not do otherwise. Equally if you have only a short entry for each meditation you are far more likely to read it again, than if you know you have reams to read. It is also a good way of making you consciously realise what you have obtained from your meditation at the time. The benefit and effects of meditation can be very precise at any one given time, as well as gradual over a prolonged time, so making short diary entries helps you to know what they are.

Who With?

Meditation can be a solitary or group experience. Many people combine both, attending a group on a regular basis and performing their own meditations privately between meetings. I have already mentioned that I encourage my students to establish a daily habit of meditating by themselves, or perhaps with a partner. So which then, is best?

This depends very much on the type of person you are and on what may be happening to you in life at any given time. If you are the kind of person who is comfortable with their own company and uncomfortable in the presence of others, you will obviously prefer solitary meditation. Consider though, in your solitude, why this may be so. Likewise if you find the inevitable noises of throat clearing, sniffing, stomach rumbling and the like that occur in any group annoying, you may find that group meditation serves only to increase your stress level, not make it manageable. You may be the kind of person that if left to your own devices will rarely, if ever, get around to implementing the discipline necessary for solitary meditation, but once place in a group are the hardest working member. You may find that knowing there are others in the room meditating away galvanises you into deeper meditation than you can achieve on your own. There are many reasons for both situations being 'better' and you must therefore decide for yourself which works for you.

One thing that experience will show you is that meditation in a group is different to meditating by yourself. My experience taught me that this is because it is easier to concentrate your mind on the subject in hand when you know within that others are doing the same thing. Each has made the same sacrifices to meet and there is therefore an element of duty each one has to all the others. We respond to that knowing within and so are more able to concentrate, producing a more effective meditation. But there is also a deeper reason why group meditation is often easier than when we try by ourselves.

We can first explain this by repeating the oft quoted maxim from Jesus in the Book of Matthew (18:20): "For where two or three are gathered in my name, there am I in the midst of them". I should explain hastily here that I am arguably taking this quote rather out of context, for in this quote I see Jesus as the Spirit, that spark of Divine, in whichever form or forms you conceive this to be (any is fine by me!). It is my belief and experience that each of us has within that same spark of the Divine, be it God, Goddess or both, or an old man on a cloud with a long, white beard. The human animal is, despite attempts to cage it in houses and cities, still a creature of instinct and responds at that instinctive level. Perhaps it is that we are also pack animals, like our friends and teacher the wolf. So when we gather to meditate in a group of two, three or seven hundred and eighty three, we can sense that Divine Spark within each of us and a collective identity takes over. Thus is established the group mind, spoken of in many esoteric schools.

By this we really mean something a little deeper than a body of people concentrating on the same subject, although this may be seen as the beginning of the group mind. We shall see as we progress through the book that our physical reality has running through, or rather underneath it, and energy force that acts like a blueprint for that reality.

This energy is actually more real than what we can see and touch before us, but more of that later. Thus far, we have only identified that this energy is Universal: it is freely available to all and shared by all, whether they know it or not. When in a group meditation, we each relax deeply ad we can sense that Divine Spark within. With this comes the recognition that we all share in this Spark or energy.

With this recognition comes a sharing of identity, knowledge and awareness. This is a powerful force, the human mind being an incredibly potent force (though little used). That power enables us to share a collective identity, which we can refer to as the group mind. By simply meeting at an agreed time for the purpose of meditation and relaxing ourselves deeply, we have opened our awareness to the others in the group and shared something of the basic animal instinct we all have and of the Spirit we all have. It is thus we are pack animals, able to generate a strong force or energy when in a group. We thus achieve a state of awareness of the equality of each person, each one being a vital part of that collective identity or group mind. Each individual's mind is separate at the conscious level, but joined at the deepest unconscious level.

This energy then exists on the group level, becoming more easily identified and felt and in turn made of stronger material the longer the group meets and is in harmony of purpose and mind. This creates a pool of resources upon which each member may draw in accordance with their need at any one time. To return then to the Bible and this time a quote of St. Paul, we are truly "Members One of Another", linked and untied by this energy. Perhaps now that this is being proven as a scientific reality in the field of quantum physics, we may learn little by little to apply this truth globally and share food, wealth, comfort and love, as well as it happening instinctively on the unseen energy level, given chance.

This fact does not make group meditation any better than solitary of course, but it does add another dimension to what can be achieved when we gather together. For those interested in this, I would refer readers to my previous book *'Taming the wolf – Full Moon Meditations'*.

On the solitary front, it is well known in esoteric schools that a prolonged period spent by oneself often gives rise to visions and revelations. It may well be that the pursuit of solitary meditation is a reflection of this mythological fact. Performed on a daily basis, a time spent in meditation alone can afford one a strength of spirit that can act as a great strength in times of trouble. It can also give one the feeling of inner strength through one's routine activities, which improves confidence, ability and efficiency.

There are therefore benefits to be had both from group and solitary meditation and both are to be recommended. When meditating in a group there are many principles it is helpful to observe, with regard to confidentiality, listening, politeness, regularity, responsibility and so on. These things and others must each be worked out and agreed upon by any group at its inception in accordance with its own objectives. These things, once clearly defined will help the group mind to become established more quickly and clearly and so will aid each individual's meditation with that group.

So we come to the end of this long chapter which sees you prepared now to begin to learn some of the techniques of meditation. There is a long way to go yet, but by faithfully reading this Chapter and absorbing its ideas and recommendations you will find that you have helped yourself enormously now it has come to the act of meditation. You will also find that you will be able to establish good habits from the outset which will enable you to sense the benefit your meditation is giving you all the quicker. So now you can relax and begin to help yourself through meditation.

Chapter 2 - Relaxation Techniques

There is a popular theory that states that before one is able to relax, one must first become aware of how tense one is. This is in order for full awareness of relaxation and what that means and feels like for each individual, to occur. In this Chapter we will look at the process of relaxation, including methods by which we can use tension to help our relaxation, following the above principle. We have already mentioned the principle that whatever we experience totally disappears and it is by this means that we are able to rid ourselves of tension and so slip effortlessly into a state of relaxation.

It must first be mentioned that we are dealing here with the specific and intentional experience of relaxation, rather than the overall degree in life to which we are relaxed. We are learning at specific times to sit or lie down and become relaxed, in order to help ourselves. In times past, this state is one that would have occurred more naturally, as would the process of meditation have been included in and part of, one's daily activities. Indeed, this is perhaps the reason for the requirement for this book and the necessity of learning meditation as a separate and distinct art, quite apart from it being a natural process included as part of one's life.

In more agricultural times of years past, our Western lives were much closer and more dependent on the seasons and annual cycle of Nature, than is presently the case. This meant hours of work sowing seeds, tending them cutting them. This in turn meant hours and hours of routine work, endlessly repeating the same tasks. In such cases it is possible for the human mind to enter a different level of consciousness. The actions of the body are taken over by the mechanics therein and the mind is left to wander where it will. This is not daydreaming, where the mind does indeed wander, aimlessly, without direction or purpose, exploring the realms of fantasy. Rather these tasks could have been carried out by the body while the mind of the person reflected on a specific subject, event, person or whatever. In this way, the task becomes the catalyst for the meditation – the exploration by the mind of whatever one wishes to concentrate upon. This allows an 'altered state of consciousness' or awareness to occur naturally and without effort. This has the natural effect of relaxing the body, for the person loses full conscious awareness of what the body is doing and so is able to relax itself, without interference from the complicated messages the mind is constantly feeding the body.

In such cases the body is able to become the perfect and amazing working machine that it is. Likewise, the mind. We use so little of our minds in our daily lives that it seems a shameful waste not to utilise the ability we have to enter another state of consciousness to help ourselves and others.

Now that we do not have a society that allows for this purpose for routine activities, we must learn how to relax properly again, as a separate and distinct task, apart from our outer lives. It is my hope that once you have acquired this 'skill' or rather habit, it will become gradually and naturally ingrained into your daily life so as to be a part of the whole of it. It is then that the general and natural state of relaxation is restored and we begin again to live our lives in a calmer and looser way.

It may seem that the nature of our Western society, work and habits, actively object to our mind switching off and being allowed to drift with a purpose held within. The onslaught of information we face, from television, radio, advertising, magazines, books, people and so on, together with the noise they generate, intrudes on our mind and its ability to slip into a different awareness.

There are certain times when our modern activities do seem to encourage this physical routine that is conducive to relaxation and meditation, some rather better than others. One example, already mentioned is that of driving, coupled with the regular speed and monotony of the actions required; often enable the mind to slip into that altered state. This is not however the ideal time for this to happen, as is the case with certain factory work, where routine and monotonous actions can be required next to powerful machinery.

A rather more beneficial and safe mechanical activity that promotes this altered state for the mind is running. As a long distance runner I view my training runs as moving meditations. The rhythm, both of running itself and breathing regularly, allow for the space my mind requires to slip away from everyday matters. It is as if it empties itself of daily thoughts, concerns and worries and is able to focus without the distraction of what my body is doing and concentrate fully and properly on what I wish it to.

Do not be alarmed however, I am not about to say that it is necessary to take up running marathons to learn how to relax and meditate – though it will help! What is clear is that the mind has this faculty and it is a natural thing. However modern society given that we spend our time dealing with all its inventions, does not allow for its natural occurrence. We must facilitate it in some other way. Hence the need for learning meditation as a separate activity.

Before we learn how to meditate we must learn how to relax. It is this state of relaxation which opens the mind up to meditation. There is often a very thin dividing line between relaxation and meditation. One way we may look at and define this difference is by seeing relaxation as a state in which we are physically calm and the mind is calm too. When we then collect and gather that state of mental calmness and focus from there on a specific subject, we could be said to be meditating. However, this is only one approach, more Western in origin and practice, to the vast subject and nature of meditation.

So let us concern ourselves with the progress of relaxation, both as an exercise with enormous benefits for our overall health and as a prelude to meditation. It is estimated that approximately two thirds of diseases are caused by stress, in one form or another. One of the most powerful and direct antidotes to stress is of course relaxation. This alone must be cause enough to include a relaxation practice amongst our daily activities, but there can be many others.

With time, we become more relaxed as our natural way of being. This allows for our actions to be more effective. (Such is the case by the way, with running – the more relaxed you are, the more effective and conservative your running will be!). Being more relaxed as a permanent state of being obviously prevents the accumulation of the deposits within the body that stress produces. In this way a daily relaxation procedure prevents dis-ease occurring in the first place. Honouring yourself and your own needs, physically, mentally, emotionally and spiritually is also a very good reason for the inclusion of relaxation times in your life. There can be many issues that may prevent this, but once established as a regular pattern you will find that you have a need to honour your needs before others. The principle here is that you can be of no use to others or the world if you are not balanced and relaxed in yourself, with your own needs and comforts addressed as best you are able at any given time.

It can be a good idea to make a list of your own reasons for needing to relax. Include in this anything that comes to you, however insignificant or ridiculous it may seem. Everything you mind gives to you will have some relevance. When writing this list, simply let your mind speak to you and write down what comes to you, without stopping to think about it first. Once don, file the list away until you have forgotten its contents. Then retrieve the list and read through it. You may surprise yourself with what you have come up with! The effect this process has is to make it seem as if someone who knows you truly is clearly stating why you need to relax. This will increase your motivation, which is sometimes necessary.

It is really only yourself that can motivate you. Others may outline the benefits of relaxation and how wonderful it feels to be relaxed, as I have hopefully done here, but all this is empty noise unless you wish to do it yourself. In the discipline of the daily practice it is ultimately only yourself and your level of motivation that is in control. There are ways, which I have already mentioned which you can make things easier for yourself, but in the end it is down to you.

This brings us back to honouring the self, for it may well be that you cannot motivate yourself to keep your relaxation practice up (or for that matter running, giving up smoking, drinking, drugs, television etc.) There is the need to honour your own needs and to realise that there is nothing more important, save not harming others, than their fulfilment. This must become an inner state of awareness in each individual and there are many blocks to this, from our past and current experience and life just happening to us.

All I can say in this book on this subject is that meditation will help dissolve those blocks and that the practice of meditation will help you long term. Whether you have it within you at this time to put that into practice is your concern. I hope that this book will open the way up for you to do this and guide and motivate you – I can do no more.

Let us now turn our attention to how to relax. Given below are two different ways in which you can achieve a state of relaxation, that are complete in themselves as well as being excellent forerunners to meditation. They can also be used independently or in combination. If used together, perform them in the order they are given here.

Tensioning

This first exercise utilises the principle we looked at earlier, of needing first to experience ones tension in order to become relaxed and also consciously aware of this. This exercise is of course just one way in which you can achieve this, but is one that I have found students respond particularly well to. The technique itself is quite simple and is best performed lying down, on your back. To begin with become aware of yourself and your body by just lying still and allowing yourself to become calm. Let your breathing settle into its own natural pattern, by simply breathing without considering it. As you relax into the exercise this will occur naturally and your breath will become shallower, which in turn helps you to relax.

Then start the Tensioning process by curling your toes down into your feet and gradually clenching them as tight as possible. Do not strain and do not jerk the muscle in a sudden motion, as this is likely to result in a torn or 'pulled' muscle. Tighten the toes as far as they will comfortably go and feel the pull across your feet. Feel the tension in your feet, inside and out. Hold this position for a few seconds. It is a good idea to hold your breath as you tighten your toes and then after a few seconds, let your toes relax and breathe out. Make the whole movement a smooth and steady one. The object here is to stretch the muscles in order to allow tension to go, nothing more.

The remainder of the exercise is a series of movements, working your way up through the body. The movements are performed in exactly the same manner as above. This is to breathe in as you make the movement, holding the breath and the muscles in position for a few seconds (perhaps count to four as you do this) then to breathe out as you release the hold. This should be one smooth and easy movement each time, performed at your own pace. Now work your way through the list of movements given below, for ease pausing for one breath in between movements, taken at the pace and level that is comfortable for you.

After your toes, point your feet away from you, as you lay down. Feel the pull in the front of your ankles and legs.

Point your feet up towards your head, where you lie. Feel this pull in the backs of your legs.

Clench the thigh muscles tightly, these are very strong and can be tightened a great deal, but do not jerk.

Clench the buttocks tightly. These muscles are tender yet strong, so hold this position tightly. Tighten the stomach muscles and feel the tension here. Feel it release also as you let go.

Make fists with your hands and feel the tension pouring into this aggressive movement. Be careful not to dig long nails into your palms, but do really feel the pull here. Let that aggression go as you let your hands relax.

Tighten your biceps (upper arm muscles). Imagine that you are showing your muscles off to an admirer to do this.

Push your shoulders back and in towards your back. Feel the pull across your chest.

Raise your shoulders and feel the tension in your shoulders themselves.

Push your head forward and feel the pull in your neck muscles.

Screw the face up as tight as you can. Clench your eyes and mouth tightly shut. No one will see what you look like if you are in a group as they will be doing the same – including the tutor. We rarely allow our faces to let go of tension so hold tightly here. It takes more muscles to frown than to smile so make life a little easier for yourself and come out of this movement with a slight smile.

Tense the whole body once or twice finally and let go in the usual manner. This will allow last areas of tension to be released.

Now just let yourself drift. Breathe easily and without effort and just take a few minutes to enjoy and be aware of what being relaxed feels like, perhaps for the very first time. If you happen to become aware of any areas in your body that still feel tense, then repeat the necessary movement to rid yourself of it.

When you have had enough of lying there, deepen your breathing a little and become aware again of where you are and what is around you.

When you are ready open your eyes and take a look around you before you stand up, to adjust your senses back to their everyday awareness. You can of course play some music to help you or to enjoy your time of drifting at the end.

You may find that you drop off to sleep, which is a food indication that you are too tense and your body needs to rest – let it, the world will still be there when you wake up.

Lastly here, if you are suffering from any muscular or skeletal problems do be gentle with your body and use your common sense.

Having learnt how to relax our bodies it is now necessary to learn how to do the same for our breathing. Breathing is of course something we all do, and do without thinking permanently. It is an instinctive act that affects us all a great deal. Without noticing it we can become tense just by watching say, a horror or thriller film, and our breathing then becomes short. When the tension depicted in the film passes we breathe out a long, deep breath, letting the tension go this way too. This you may think is the mark of a good film, to make you react in this way, but do learn to be aware when you are responding like this and use such techniques as those given below to prevent your body becoming knotted up with tension. There are many other circumstances in which we react similarly to this – visiting the doctor, dentist, job interview, exams, solicitors etc. How many can you think of that you have done recently and responded like this?

If you learn to be more aware of your breathing and how you are doing it, you are taking the first step to gaining some degree of control over it. Since this is an instinctive act, it follows that it can have a huge effect on your overall state of being. By being able to control the effect your breath has on you, you can prevent the automatic installation of stress patterns in your life and calm yourself prior to the interview, dentist etc. These are specific examples but the prevention of stress also applies generally in your body and your life. Overall you will become a more relaxed person, more free flowing and in control once you become a more relaxed person, more free flowing and in control once you have become aware of and in control of your breathing.

There are many techniques to achieve this and again I am simply offering two that I know from experience work. These techniques are also excellent preparations or introductions to entering a full state of meditation. They can be used to take you deeper and deeper in to a state of relaxation, in which case they really become meditations in themselves, since they provide the perfect state for your mind to objectively focus on one subject, image or whatever.

The Fourfold Breath

Both these techniques are again very simple and very effective. It is perhaps their simplicity that makes them so effective. As with the majority of such breathing techniques, they rely on establishing a rhythm to which you submit your breathing pattern, for their successful working. All that the technique consists of is as per its title – your breath becomes fourfold. That is, you count to a count of four each time that you breathe in. You then count to another count of four whilst breathing out. Then just repeat the same count breathing in again and then count to four again breathing out and so on.

Make the count silently to yourself and do not concern yourself with how long it takes you to count to four. Your breathing and counting will adjust themselves to what is a comfortable level for you, after the first few breaths. All you should concentrate on is your counting and your breathing, nothing more. Ensure that you are not straining your breath too shallow or too deeply, but just breathe smoothly and evenly.

52

It is not the count but the rhythm that is important here and it is this that relaxes you. Allow yourself to find your own natural rhythm. We ALL have rhythm, however tone deaf or bad a dancer we may be – we all have a heart-beat, so we all have rhythm. It is within us and is natural and above all, without effort and so relaxed. Use this to relax your breath too and enter a deeper state of relaxation than ever before.

As you continue to count and breathe to that fourfold rhythm, gently let the counting go and let the rhythm remain. With your eyes closed you can sink into a deep state of relaxation that is infinitely calming and comforting. There can be a very womb-like feel to your own rhythm which is a wonderful experience. Perform this technique for as long as you wish. It is effective in just a few short minutes, but in certain of the aforementioned circumstances may take longer to calm you. Have patience in these cases, it *will* work.

The fourfold Breath can be performed anywhere without anyone knowing – on the bus, or train, outside the interview room, as exam papers are being dealt. It is not necessary to close one's eyes, as all that is important is the rhythm and your breathing. Once you have become proficient at this technique you will find that you are able to switch into it with a minimum of counting, just to remind you of your own natural rhythm and off you go. It is really so easy to establish this control and it can have so many benefits for you in everyday life.

The Four-Two Breath

This technique is very similar to the Fourfold Breath but has a slight variation to the breathing pattern. It if offered as an alternative to the above. In some people the breathing pattern of four may be limiting or their mind may begin to wander very quickly. If you know that you are prone to a wandering mind and unable to concentrate without difficulty, this exercise will make your meditation easier if you use it as an introduction each time for a few minutes. It will also have the same stress and anxiety reducing effects as the Fourfold Breath. It is simply that some will find this technique more effective, others not.

The technique is the same in all respects as the Fourfold Breath except that you hold your breath for a count of two between the in and out breaths that still last for the count of four. This may feel slower to some people who are perhaps more stressed at any time and so may take a little more time and effort to become calm. Again, do not force the breathing in any way and allow a natural rhythm to the overall effect to take its place. You will need to concentrate a little harder to use this technique, but as we will see in the next Chapter, this is of great use when entering meditation.

Again perform this technique for as long as you wish or as long as feels necessary. After just a few minutes you will notice the benefits as your breathing will be under your control instead of it controlling you and having you at its mercy to be affected by every little thing that comes along.

We have now explored ways in which we can become relaxed. These techniques are complete in themselves and can justly be called meditations if performed in a deep and concentrated manner. They are just as effective however when performed in the situations described above and others similar. They are best performed and most effective when you do not try too hard. This can be a useful closing maxim for this Chapter – that the more you try to meditate the harder it becomes. Remember this as we now enter into our exploration of some basic meditations.

Chapter 3 - Grounding and Connecting

We have now crossed that vague and blurred line that divides relaxation and meditation in many people's minds. We are now suitable prepared and free to begin our exploration of the inner worlds, wherein dwell all manner of demons and kings, wolves and wizards that symbolise our inner selves and other realms. This book however, is less concerned with the use of meditation as an exploratory map through those worlds and more with its use in helping you through your working day.

We have already looked at the many practicalities that must be considered before we can use the practice of meditation successfully on a regular basis. Just as with food it is necessary to vary the diet occasionally in order to keep our taste buds alive and enjoyment of our food at an optimum level, it is preferable to vary one's practice of meditation from time to time, instead of coming to mechanically repeat the same dry procedure each day.

The human mind would soon become bored with this practice and invent distractions to keep you from meditating. Before long, you miss the occasional day and the breaks grow longer, because you simply don't want to meditate as it is not a productive or enjoyable activity. In part for this reason I have included through the remaining Chapters of this book many meditations that you can try, that can keep you occupied for many moons.

Prior to this however, we must learn the essential method of how to enter that meditative state and condition, that is rightly called meditation itself. Without this, we are merely building a world within that is frail and brittle, waiting to be destroyed with the first challenge and difficulty that occurs. The basic and rather obvious wisdom of building a secure foundation before you build the house itself applies here.

I will say at the outset of this explanation however, that this is no mere introduction technique and that alone. Used properly it can become a deep and powerful exercise that each time it is performed takes you deeper and deeper within, or above. It has become the mainstay of my daily practices since I was first taught a form of it many years ago.

Looking back I can see that it has grown and adapted itself as I have grown and changed over those years, serving to maintain the vital contact with my inner self that guides me on my own path through life. Without this, I feel that I would still be treading a maze of what I now refer to as my previous life. It is thanks to this Grounding and Connecting technique that I am able to now say I have discovered myself and learnt a little of why I am here.

Grounding and Connecting then is vital. Without this technique, or one of its many different variations and forms, the student or practitioner of meditation effectively opens themselves to danger each time they meditate. Just why this is so we shall see, but for now let us explain exactly what we mean by Grounding and Connecting.

To do this we must return to the concept and idea of energy that we dealt with briefly in Chapter 1. There, we saw that we are united by this energy or life force at a group level by concentration and the power of thought. This idea we must now dissect.

The exciting practice and study that is labelled 'quantum physics' is now giving credence to what occultists and mystics the world over have been saying for thousands of years. This is basically (and infinitely more simply than books on quantum physics'!) that the Universe consists of and is linked, like a spider's web, by threads or particles of energy. Encoded within each particle of energy is effectively a complete Universe of its own, which is absorbed into ours and so manifests as the everyday, tangible reality we experience around us.

We will see in the following Chapter how this principle can be extended to enable us to obtain what we need in our lives, but for now we use the idea to provide us with our stable and effective means of meditating, which is Grounding and Connecting. This in turn, follows the now proven and accepted idea that 'energy follows thought'. The energy that follows our thoughts is the same stuff that as quantum physics obligingly shows, is the stuff of life itself, the very force of life. It is from this life-force that our world and reality derives.

What we think then, is constructed of this life force or energy. Our thoughts are alive and once having come into our minds effectively flow out into the Universe, where they become something real. This may cause you to think that it is vital to think no negative or bad thought. But we cannot avoid our instinct, which causes us to think without pausing to consider what reality this is going to result in! The likes of Dale Carnegie and other exponents of positive thinking must accept that the human being is still an animal and therefore instinctive, with immediate responses, that in one sense, are out of our control. Rather we can modify the general state or condition of our minds to be more content and lead a life that brings us to a level of satisfaction that helps to remove the need for bad or negative thought, whether instinctive or not.

The practice of Grounding and Connecting is, in this western approach to meditation, the key procedure for achieving what may sound like a nice idea but unreal. It is very real, and indeed more real than the chair which you are sitting on and the book you hold in your hand. This realm of energy transcends and outlives your body, your house and all your possessions. For it operates at a level that is beyond time, where that which is reality is that which we think.

So when we are able to achieve a state of awareness or consciousness in which we can feel, perceive and interact with this consciousness in which we feel, perceive and interact with this energy or life force, we can learn to shape our lives and reality to be the way we want them to be. It is for this reason that we must Ground and Connect, each and every time we meditate, for this is a big responsibility, where we can at last, take full responsibility not just for ourselves and our own lives, but for the Earth and Universe that give us those lives in the first place.

We have seen then how to relax and it is this physical relaxation that allows the mind the freedom to explore deeper levels than it is usually allowed to, it having so many other trivialities to concentrate on in the body. Once this is removed, something of the real potential of the mind can be accessed. At this deeper level, we can sense and feel the movement and flow of that life force and energy that is, as we have seen, the blueprint for life itself. It is like being handed the map that shows you how you are made and what you will do in life, before you begin it. You can now make any adjustments that you wish and plot the course you would like to take through your life.

History shows us however that the human is not a wise animal and is bound to make mistakes. Indeed, it is in those mistakes that we should learn to progress. We need guidance and we need help, that much is clear. If we are left to our own devices, we invariably get it wrong, whatever 'it' is. This applies both as a species and to each individual within that species. Grounding and Connecting is the method by which we can obtain that guidance and ensure we do not lead ourselves 'up the garden path'.

When we become deeply relaxed, it could be argued that it is the focussed concentration of our thoughts that takes us into meditation. What we concentrate our thoughts on is of course, entirely up to us. The point here being that you become immersed in your contemplation, or perhaps follow a guided journey so fully that you are actually in that place, which when you consider the principle that energy follows thought and life comes from that energy, is true.

So it becomes necessary and vital to have some means by which you can find your way back to the everyday world of our conscious minds. This method is Grounding.

Grounding

Grounding has other benefits and uses as well. The term 'grounding' is a big clue as to what is actually happening here. What you are doing when you perform the grounding part of the complete technique is that you are joining or linking your own life force, energy or essence with the Earth.

The Earth supports and upholds each and every living thing on and in it. It is perhaps for this reason that the Earth as a living being is called Mother, for like all Mothers, She gives constantly to her children – us. We have been entrusted by whatever powers that you view to be to look after the Earth as She looks after us. If the balance goes, we're in trouble.

Grounding then, joins your life force with the body and then at a deeper level, the life force of the Earth. This is just as if, like a plant, or tree, you take root in the soil and so depend for your stability, health and well-being on the Earth and on that connection.

When you are able to link with the Earth on a daily basis, you become gradually and instinctively more aware of your dependency on the Earth and of your intrinsic connection with all things. You realise then what shamans the world over once knew and still know, that you are part of the rocks, stones, air, soil, trees and all creatures, as they are part of you. The Earth is that which binds these together and supports all life, including yours.

The method by which you become grounded is simply to focus your thoughts, once you have become relaxed, on your own life force moving down through your feet, through the surface you are on and down into the Earth itself. This is then returned, like for like, from the Earth into you. A full transcript of this procedure will follow this explanation, so that you can perform this vital exercise with confidence and ease. We are simply utilising that same principle of 'energy follows thought'.

With your grounding safely in place, you are able to travel wherever your mind, or your meditation teacher, wishes to take you, safe in the knowledge that you can come back again. It is very often the case with our beloved 'floater' that they are simply not grounded.

Spending much time in so-called meditation, they never quite seem to fully take up full possession of their bodies afterwards. In meditation, one needs to be able to access that inner world, deeper or higher state of awareness, do what one wishes to do and then return, fully and completely, to the mundane world, enriched and enlivened with what one has experienced, learnt and realised. Without grounding or some form of it, this is not possible.

What occurs instead of once that the switch to those other levels is made, nothing is real or concrete and the mind is set free like a mischievous child to play what pranks it may. Given ever deeper scope as the meditator progresses, all sorts of fantasies and revelations occur until one believes themselves the subject of some special Divine providence. There are many of them about!

It is perhaps worth pointing out here the dangers of meditating (at a deep level) without grounding. On your return you would find yourself somewhat drained and tired. This feeling tends not to go away and even after prolonged sleep you would find that you just cannot shake the feeling off. You also would become extremely sensitive to noises around you, and also to the input of information that you receive. This would result in your mind being constantly invaded by a stream of unchecked, unwanted information that would overload your systems. The eventual result is exhaustion and breakdown. This may sound extremist and exaggerated, but it is not.

It may be useful to mention here that for the purposes of healing, the same is true. Healers often complain of feeling drained after working. This is largely because the energy they are transmitting to their patient comes from them, not through them. In order to make themselves a channel for this force and power, it is necessary to perform some form of grounding and connecting.

Once firmly grounded, we can explore to the farthest reaches of our Universe and even beyond. We can travel through time, forward and back and still return unharmed and strong, to the present moment, just as we left it. Of course we need to know where we are going and that we will not get lost en-route and this is why, equal to our grounding, we need to perform our Connecting.

Connecting

As we have established that the life force we deal with in grounding is in and of the Earth as well as ourselves, so it is also in and of the Universe, as that which is above and all round us. We can look at this as the Earth Force gives and promotes and upholds life, whilst the Universe guides and directs life, both individual and collective. Thus we arrive at the maxim 'As above, so below', quoted in so many esoteric manuals. Here we have a direct experience of that principle, unique to each individual and yet in essence the same the world over.

Once in meditation we need to know that we can journey and explore in our minds anywhere we wish, knowing without any shade of doubt that our imaginations will not run off with our consciousness and tell us that we are in fact a visitor from a planet that has been nestling unnoticed behind Mars all these years! We need to know that the wanderings and subsequent realisations in our minds whilst we meditate are real, worthwhile and of some practical use and application.

We also need to know that our meditations are taking us to a genuinely higher level of awareness and consciousness, as opposed to opening us to the deeper, darker levels of ourselves, or to a falsehood of childhood conditioning or other's influence and opinion that shapes us. We need a direct link and channel to our 'Higher Self' as it is this that will serve us unconditionally and will always give us truth, pleasant or not. This Higher Self can be looked on as the part of us that knows what we need, as opposed to what we want. It is the part of us that is, if you will, part spirit and part human. It has a permanent link and connection to the Divine, whilst also being able to relate the product, of that link to the conscious mind, through the medium of meditation. As such it is the higher source of life itself. It is that to which we can reach for guidance, confirmation and healing. As a force that is in essence unconditional love, it brings healing, cleansing and purification. When in meditation we connect ourselves with this Universal life force, we receive a side effect that is this healing. This sets in motion a chain reaction in our minds and bodies that affords us the opportunity and brings us to a closer awareness of who and what we truly are and can be, if we live up to our full potential.

If we see this force and power as the energy flow we have already identified exists within the Earth we can see that with our thoughts we can allow a flow of energy from ourselves, above the head, to move up and connect with that Universal force. As such we put ourselves in touch with Creation itself. We are part of that creation and 'Connecting' is the conscious experience of this. Just as astrologers view the principles of the planets affecting us with their own particular energy or life force, so here we are connecting, in one sense, with a combination of all those energies and forces. Together they form a holistic whole, greater than the sum of its parts, that is the force and energy of creation. It is really but a simple task to use the principle that energy follows thought to make ourselves aware of this, on a daily basis, through the meditation that follows.

The procedure for Connecting is rather like that of Grounding, but going up, rather than down. By focussing on the flow of grounding energy moving up through your body you are able to allow your level of awareness to rise. Moving this above your head you can begin to feel lighter and feel as if you have frown in height. This is simply the energy flow moving up. If you then switch your thoughts to the flow of life force and energy that flows throughout infinity and the Universe, you begin to attract to yourself a concentrated 'dose' of it down to your being and your body. By focussing your concentration on this life force moving down, you can feel its cleansing, healing and guiding power flowing through you. This connects you with the Universe and with your own self in truth. With this connection comes an awareness of your inner thoughts and intuition.

Once you have allowed this to flow down you will sense and feel within that the two energies and forces, from below and above, are blending and joining. Allow this to happen for it happens at a place that is truly the very centre of your own being. You can now sense who you truly are and feel your intrinsic connection with all living things, great and small. This gives a wonderful feeling of balance and well-being that is hard to describe and needs to be experienced by each individual. Once experienced however, it alters the self and you will never be quite the same.

With its awareness comes a sense of inner peace that is the mainstay of a satisfied and content life. It will not take all your problems away of course but it will give you the means by which to view them from a safe and objective place. For myself, it is what keeps me together and assures me that there is 'more to life than this'. It is this one place, awareness and experience, accessed on a daily basis that enables me to be at peace with myself and the world. From this centre I know that I can cope with whatever the world sees fit to launch at me and can find peace despite the horrors around me. Grounding and Connecting also enables me to have a conscious awareness of the Spirit that dwells within me and to which I constantly strive.

Being connected then allows for the mind to cease from its endless everyday chatter. It allows for peace of emotion and we are able to let go of the defences we carry with us. In that place of peace we can finally know truth, as it exists at that moment.

Having performed your Grounding and Connecting your reach this state of inner balance and the peace comes to you from knowing that everything is just as it should be. It is in this state and awareness that you can be said to be 'centred'. This is another term, like energy, that is over used in many places without a true understanding of what it is and what it means. Being centred is the product of being grounded and connected.

Once this becomes a regular, daily practice you will find that you have a greater overall awareness and control over yourself and your life. This takes time to establish itself in the pattern of your make up, but will once acquired, permeate the whole of your thoughts, feelings and actions. You operate then from a place of truth and peace, knowing rather than believing or hoping that what you are doing is the right thing. Thus being grounded and connected (Centred) becomes a general state of being. You can then use your daily practice to ensure that you remain in balance and in control, and live life in a balanced and measured way, free from extremes, of thought, word or deed that would seek to pull you apart. It is true indeed that 'all things in moderation' is a good principle to live by, or put another way, more appealing way, 'a little of what you fancy does you good'!

There are many indications happening on an instinctive level in your life that can tell you, you are ungrounded or disconnected. These too can become a guide to ensure that the path you are treading is leading in the direction that you would wish or that is intended for you.

If you are ungrounded you may find yourself unknowingly pleasing others to the detriment of your own well-being. The ability to say an honest 'no' when you need to is not unkind – you must first be kind to yourself before you can be kind to others. Often this can escalate into illness and the ungrounded person is one who will have frequent colds, tiredness, listlessness and apathy. Loss of temper can become an easy habit as well as clumsiness, with words as well as objects (including your own body). The ungrounded person always seems to be in a rush for they do not have the inner awareness that knows things will get done in their own good time, just like the tortoise in the race against the hare. Keep your grip on reality and you have no need to worry over the future and can live fully awake and aware in the present moment.

Grounding then increases your grip on 'reality' and gives you a sense of being part of the world, with a meaningful role to play, as in fact we all do. What that role is we must discover for ourselves and meditation is one means by which to discover that role. Performed on a daily basis grounding and connecting can be the means for this, which needs to be done as we move through the natural changes circumstances and life brings. Being connected to that higher awareness is vital to the understanding of the 'plan' for us.

If you are unconnected, you may well find that you have no sense of why you are doing things, but end up doing them for the sake of it. It is rather like climbing a mountain because it is there. There is no objective in this, no calm and measured outlook or explicable reason. Once connected to one's higher purpose the mountain comes to represent a symbolic climb against adversity perhaps, or physical challenge or whatever. With the higher connection comes an awareness of knowing you are in the right place at the right time, not by accident, but by design.

Grounding and Connecting

To begin this meditation, sit or lie comfortably as you have chosen. Become settled and when you feel ready to, close your eyes. Now take a deep breath, holding the breath for a moment or two. As you breathe out, allow the tension to flow out from your body also. Take another deep breath in the same way if you feel the need. Now just allow your breath to fall into its own natural pattern, without straining in any way.

Turn your attention inwards and leave behind all the activity from your day. Let yourself be aware only of this time and this place. Allow all your thoughts and all your emotions to exist by themselves for a time, letting the world spin by itself. Detach yourself in your awareness from your cares and worries, existing instead in the present moment and place. Be aware that all that exists is yourself, here and now. Allow your thoughts to move through your mind without holding on to them at all and just letting them flow through your mind.

Let go of your feelings now and of your thoughts. All that is left is your breath. Be with this for a short time and then let this go too. Breathe easily and freely, without effort or awareness at all. From here you can begin to sense and be aware of the life force and energy that exists within your body and within your being. Allow yourself to feel its movements and flow throughout your body. Notice its direction and any differences that may exist in particular areas of your-self.

Do not try to sense this for the more you try the harder it is. Instead allow yourself to sense it, by simply being aware of yourself as a being of more than just physical body, but of energy too. This is the essential life force that exists in all living things.

Begin now to take control over the direction of that life force with your mind, remembering that 'energy follows thought'. Focus your mind and your concentration on your feet and feel them relaxing as you do so. This makes them sink firmly on to the floor. Let the floor support your weight fully, relaxing away any last areas of tension or pain.

Feel the floor support your body completely. Focus on the energy gathering in your feet. Be aware of any responses you may have to the flow of the energy, such as tingling, heat or cold. Do not react to these sensations but merely be aware of them. You may or may not sense these sensations – there is no merit attached to them either way.

Now extend your awareness out below the soles of your feet and imagine that the life force and energy moves with your thoughts. As the energy follows your thoughts, so you begin to have an awareness and sensation of moving down. Imagine that you are taking root, just like a plant or a tree. The life force moves down then, through the foundations of any building you are in and on joining with the Earth and taking root within its body. Let the Earth begin to support you instead of supporting yourself.

Focus on the energy below you now, moving deeper and deeper down in to the soil and rocks of the Earth. Feel the structure of the Earth beneath you and let this support you. Imagine that the tips of your toes stretch deep down into the soil and feel the warmth surrounding you. Begin now to absorb the goodness from the Earth into your own body. Feel the minerals and nutrients that promote and strengthen your life force seeping up and into your body. Mentally draw in that goodness, freely given by the Earth. Be aware of the heaviness of your body and feel it being strengthened as your grounding connection is made with the Earth. Let the grounding become firmly and clearly established in your awareness and in your body. Feel the safety and security of this seeping into you. Give yourself to the Earth from within, letting the ample goodness and strength hold you up and give you life. Become dependent on the Earth completely. Deep in the Earth now, you may begin to sense the pulse, becoming one with it. In this you merge and blend with that pulse, becoming one with it. In this you join now with the very essence of the Earth and the two become one.

With your grounding in place and firm now, you begin to sense that life force and Earth energy rising up into your body. Without changing your breathing in any way, draw that energy up as you next breath in, feeling it climb into your fee. Feel that strong and almost solid life force coming up through the soles of your feet and up through your body. As the Earth energy rises, you may sense yourself becoming stronger and more alive within. Do not react to any of these areas of awareness or sensations you may feel, but simply note them and continue.

Allow the Earth energy to flow further and further up through your body. Feel it permeating your body, inside and out. As it flows up through you, feel the strength, warmth and vitality flooding through you too. Be aware of this life force moving up through your bones, through each of your veins, your muscles and over your skin too, touching every part of you and covering it with this strong force of life. Let this energy hold you in your position and become dependent on it.

Let this grounding energy rise then, until you sense that it covers you completely. Let it continue to rise until it covers your head. Feel yourself as a being of the Earth, grounded firmly into the body of the Earth. Let this be your stability and your whole awareness for a few moments as you pause to adjust yourself to this feeling and this knowledge.

Now begin to focus your concentration on the crown of your head. Fix your attention on a point in the centre and at the top of your head, just lightly touching the surface. As you focus here feel the energy flowing into this area of your body and your being. Feel the lightness in your awareness here and let yourself become accustomed to this.

Become aware now of the energy and life force from above, flowing down to all living things, to the Earth itself, and to you. Let yourself be conscious of its lightness and its feel. Imagine this higher life force flowing down from the Universe into your own being, through the crown of your head. Feel this force and energy flowing from infinity, down to you. In this, let yourself be connected to the Universe and to this source of life and creation itself.

As you focus on this higher energy you can feel your awareness and level of consciousness rise. Be aware of the lightness of your body and of the higher aspects to you. You may notice some of the sensations above you now, about your head and on your forehead. Let this tingling heat or cold simply be part of you and feel the higher life force connecting you clearly and firmly to the Universe, to your own higher guidance and to life itself.

Now begin to feel this Universal life force flowing smoothly down into your body. Imagine and sense its movement downwards from above, through the crown of your head. Feel its healing and cleansing flow coming down within and without your body and being. Feel it healing you as it goes, cooling and guiding you. Let yourself be connected to this energy, to yourself and to the truth of your own existence.

Let this higher energy become a part of you and you become more and more connected to it. Feel it move down through your neck and over your shoulders and arms. Feel it flow down through your body now, enclosing and permeating every organ within. In this way you become a being, aware more of energy than of body. Let this sensation and awareness settle and become clear.

Now become aware of the Earth energy from below merging and blending with that higher energy from above. Feel the balance of these two forces, holding you upright, supporting you, giving you life and guiding you. As they blend and balance each other, so they balance you. Become aware now of the balance that lies at the very centre and heart of your being. The energy of the Earth meets the energy of the Universe in this place where there is perfect peace and perfect balance. Experience the very centre of your being now and let yourself become fully aware of this.

Take time now to let yourself float and drift in this place, where all things meet and there is infinite possibility. In this place you can discover truth, healing, peace and freedom. Let yourself rest, grounded below and connected above. Let yourself be supported by the Earth and guided by the Universe. Allow yourself to rest in the arms of the Universe and float, adrift on an endless sea of perfect calm. If you wish seek any guidance you may be in need of at this time or simply let yourself float wherever you seem to go, for a time.

When you are ready, slowly and gradually become conscious of that place of balance and of the centre of your being and body once more. Become aware then of your breathing and notice how shallow it has become. Gently and easily deepen the level of your breathing, as you do so, slowly adjusting to be aware of your body once more. Increase the level of your breath back to its usual level for you and be aware of where you are sitting or lying and of your surroundings. Take as long as you need and ensure that you make your return fully and completely. Wiggle your toes to make yourself aware of your body if you feel lightheaded still. When you are ready, let your eyes open and return.

Having read through the script above you may be thinking that it is impossible to remember all this through your meditation and you would be right. Remember though that the principles of this technique are very simple. It is simply to be aware of your own life force, then grounding this by sending it down to the Earth and letting it rise. Then draw the energy of the Universe down through you and come to a point of balance at the centre of yourself. Drift here for as long as you wish then return fully.

The script is given here in depth so that it is complete and so that you are able to learn it at the requisite depth for its maximum effect. As you progress with the technique you will find that the time it takes to perform becomes shorter and shorter, until you are able to feel yourself grounding and connecting in just a few or a couple of minutes. As such, grounding and connecting needs to become a technique that is the opening to each and every meditation that you perform, as explained previously.

Once you have become familiar with this technique then you can move on, but otherwise I recommend that you persist with this same meditation until you can do it in under five minutes (though remember that it is not a race against the clock!). The process of learning grounding and connecting will do wonders for your approach and experience in future meditations, so it is time and effort that is very well spent. It is for this reason that in future meditations given in this book, I have simply given the words of GROUND AND CONNECT at the beginning of each meditation, and where appropriate GOUND at the end. These worlds indicate that you must ground and connect yourself before you begin the meditation given in the text.

For those with a partner to share their meditation experiences, it is possible to perform a light and gentle massage technique which has a similar effect to grounding and connecting. Starting at the neck, stroke one hand gently down the spine. As this reaches the base of the spine, repeat the same movement with the other hand. This creates a continuous movement which feels like water trickling down your back, in a most pleasurable way.

On an energy level, this has the effect of shooting energy the length of the spine, making you aware of the centre of balance at your centre. The movement should be rhythmic and can be continued for as long as you feel is necessary. I am indebted to Margaret Pilling for introducing me to this lovely technique and for allowing me to reproduce it here for the benefit of others.

This grounding and connecting technique will of itself last you a lifetime. You will find that in the early stages you should allow yourself at least twenty minutes to work through it fully. At this depth and level you can continue just performing this technique and you will find that you reach a deeper or higher level each time, bit by bit. As such I commend it to you with my own personal assurance that it is a mainstay of my own meditation practice and gives me that daily awareness and connection that I need to keep me going.

Chapter 4 – Energy Meditations

Through the process of Grounding and Connecting we have seen how the basic life force or energy that exists in all living beings can be used to great effect in meditation. In this Chapter we will examine and explore how we can utilise this effect to help ourselves.

This is a book of practical meditations, where we use the art and practice of meditation to help ourselves in our daily life. As such we must look to the root causes and influences that go to create that everyday life and make it what it is. These root causes are energies, influences from our DNA and beyond, invisible to the casual observer, yet measurable and real. The acceptance of this now scientific fact is vital to the successful working of the meditations included in this Chapter. It is not enough to simply read this book, accept what is presented here and do the meditations expecting them to change you and your life. Neither is it enough to believe with faith that energy exists, trusting that my words on this page will convince you.

Rather each person must have their own experience of this energy and see for themselves that it is real, it does exist and how it feels to them. The Grounding and Connecting meditation from the previous Chapter should give you this experience. It is partly for this reason that I recommend so strongly that you stay with this exercise until you are able to repeat the procedure in full in just a few minutes.

When you are able to do this, you should KNOW within yourself that this energy exists in every fibre of your body and your being. If you do not as yet know that this is truth and applies to you equally as to every other living being in the Universe, then stick with the Grounding and Connecting until you can truly say you know this without a moment's doubt or hesitation.

This certainty is necessary because it is upon this very principle that the majority of the meditation techniques given in the book operate. The degree to which they work and are successful is of direct relation to the degree of certainty you have about the reality that energy precedes physical, tangible reality.

Once you have grasped this with the essence of your being it is also, necessary to know equally the truth that 'energy follows thought'. This is because it is the focus and directed action of your thoughts during your meditation that cause the new reality you are trying to create through it. This will not work or happen if you have any doubt or your mind wanders during the formation of that reality. Come to the stage then when you know that the energy of your thoughts during your meditation dictates its relevance and success in your life. Until this time, just keep grounding and connecting.

This energy exists then as a blueprint for our everyday, mundane lives. From this blueprint we move and have our beings. We arise from this on dimensional sheet to exist in a three dimensional world. Where then do our thoughts fit in to this map, if they create what we experience? Perhaps it is that our thoughts are the second dimension, a template for the results of those thoughts. It follows then that we need a method of controlling our thoughts so that we project into that third dimension the best and most propitious existence for ourselves. That method is 'Practical meditation'.

This life force or energy has a direct influence on every aspect of our lives. It follows that if we direct our attention within meditation to the state of condition of that energy itself, so we receive a better quality energy from which to shape ourselves and our lives. The meditations in this Chapter broadly concern themselves with this.

Energy Breath

The first of these techniques is called the Energy Breath and we can take the above definition of energy as being applicable here as well as seeing it in its more conventional sense. This technique enables you to generate a strong, stable and positive energy flow via your breath. This in turn creates energy, a feeling of well-being and positivity to enhance your motivation and vitality in life. This of course is essential to the fulfilment of your potential in whatever you do.

This meditation is then rather like ensuring that you have the correct force or enough power to start your engine and keep it going for as long as you require. There is little point in doing anything in life if it cannot be finished. The maxim 'if a thing's worth doing it's worth doing well' also applies here. This technique gives you the means to do what you are doing well and to the very best of your ability. It allows for a concentrated effort and decisiveness in your approach to life that sets you apart from the group. Though not competitive, it is as well to show that you can do something and do it well if you wish to get on in life. This technique will help you.

The Energy Breath is also good to perform if you are run down, tired or simply need an extra boost for whatever reason. It is a technique that is easy to master and can again be performed in any situation, without anyone knowing. It is in part a variation on the Fourfold and Four-Two Breaths we have already seen, though a little harder.

The breathing involved can produce a little strain so do approach this technique gently and be sensible and stay within the capabilities of what is comfortable for you. Meditation was not meant to be a struggle and should ideally be effortless. The aim with the Energy Breath is not only to breathe effortlessly but to do all things without effort. This means moving with the natural flow of that life force with is truly your being. The Energy Breath technique allows you to generate a strong, bright and clear natural flow to go with.

In terms of everyday health, the Energy Breath will increase circulation, helping as it does many secondary conditions that can arise as a result of this, such as chilblains. The technique also promotes warmth and a few minutes of this done while waiting for the bus or train on a frosty morning will help far more than getting impatient and worrying about being late.

You will find that on an overall level you will also be more awake and alert, which an increased perception. The Energy Breath is excellent if you are tired and need to stay awake, for instance on a long drive, or during studying. As it promotes a new strength and energy through your system, so do you respond to that energy. This means that all of your senses receive a boost and so you are more aware and more capable.

The technique itself is best done sitting comfortably or lying down, with your eyes closed, though this is not advisable in some circumstances (whilst driving!). Relax as best you can, then begin.

Take a moment to be aware of your state of being. Pause and allow your senses to speak to you, becoming aware of how you are, and what your needs are at this time.

Your breathing will now be quite shallow and happening by itself without effort. Be aware of where you are breathing from and adjust this if necessary so that you are breathing from your stomach rather than your chest. Now deepen your breath a little, without straining. Take your time with the exercise, there is no rush.

When you feel ready begin to count your breath. As you begin the count, breathe in until you have counted to about ten. This may be a little more it may be a little less. The exact number does not matter. It is important to take a good breath as this is what generates the force of energy required. The number will vary depending on your state of health and fitness at the time. Do not be over adventurous and take it easy. As you increase your energy so you will find that you can increase your breathing.

Having breathed in for a count of ten, twelve or so, now hold the breath for a count of about three, four or five, depending on the length of your in breath. Next, breathe out for the same count as you breathed in, whether ten, twelve or whatever. Then hold your breath in (three or four etc.) Then simply repeat this procedure for as long as you wish, with a recommended time being between ten and fifteen minutes, proceeding easily and steadily for you. When you have finished let your breathing relax again and remain for a moment, relaxing like this. Become aware of your state of being now, noticing any changes in your senses and your attitude to your needs. Ground your energy once more and finish.

The technique then is as follows:

Ground and connect

Pause to consider your needs

Breathe in (ten to twelve)

Hold breath in (three to four)

Breathe out (ten to twelve)

Hold breath out (three to four)

Repeat for 10 to 15 minutes.

Pause to reconsider your needs

Ground.

It is important not to strain your breathing in this exercise. The object is to increase energy, not to use it up and this is what will happen if you try to prove how long you can breathe for. This will result in your being breathless and little else. Do be careful when you have finished for a prolonged period spent breathing in this way will cause you to be a little light headed. Remember that it is the rhythm of the breath that is of importance and this should be relaxed and easy. Maintain a relaxed concentration and you will receive the maximum benefit from this valuable exercise.

Recharging Exercise

Another exercise designed to assist you in promoting and then maintaining an optimum flow of energy, which as we know is vital to health and effective living, is the Recharging Exercise. This focuses more on the movement and flow of energy itself, as opposed to its resultant generation through the breath. The benefits described above for the Energy Breath all apply here, and this technique could be considered a little more advanced than that.

The Recharging Exercise also takes your experience of energy a little deeper so that you are able to feel it working through your body, at its different levels. This introduces you to the existence and operation of the energy body, which we shall explore fully in the next chapter. This technique is also good to perform after a day of strenuous work or activity, when you are in need of a boost and also to help you gain a greater awareness and more control over your body.

The Recharging Exercise also introduces you to the idea of energy as colour, which gives it a different nature dependent on that colour. This will be explored fully in a later Chapter but for now all we need to know is that gold and silver between them give us a balanced identity.

The techniques can again be performed sitting or lying down, whichever you prefer. Ground and connect as usual and spend a moment to become relaxed and aware of your state of being. To do this, just ask yourself with an open minded 'How am I', and let the answers come to you. Focus on any particular needs you feel you have at this time. Now establish a steady rhythm and pattern to your breath, without placing too much emphasis on the importance of this. An easy, natural flow is what is needed, nothing more.

Now when you next breathe in, imagine and try to allow yourself to sense that you are breathing in the force, quality and energy of the gold colour from your head, down through to your feet. Imagine this flowing down each time that you breathe in. Continue this for seven breaths until you feel that gold colour has flooded your entire body from the head down. Now repeat and reverse the procedure, this time breathing in silver, with its attendant qualities and energy, from your feet, up to the top of your head. Continue breathing silver in for seven breaths.

Now focus your mind on your feet, placing your point of focus and your concentration firmly to your feet. Be aware only of your feet as you next breathe in; allow your mind to rise up into your knees. Remember that your breath itself is an energy and a focussed breath taken in this way creates an energy equal to that focus. So as you breathe in and your attention rises from your feet to your knees, draw the energy that follows your thought up to your knees also.

Take three breaths in this way, moving up in your awareness and energy from your feet to your knees each time. Between these three 'energy breaths' just relax as you breathe out. Next you take three breaths from your knees, rising up with your mind and concentration, with the energy, to your hips. Take three breaths moving up to this level each time and relaxing as you breathe out each time.

On the next breath, you move up from the Base of your spine to your abdomen, moving up to a point just below the navel. Take three breaths in the same way as before. You then move up from the navel to the solar plexus, situated just below the rib cage. Take your time with each of three breaths for each stage as each one is dependent on the one before, to rise up with equal strength and energy in turn. Move up now from the solar plexus to the heart and

78

then from your heart to your throat, this accurately being the base of your neck, no higher. Breathe three breaths in for each level, drawing energy in each time as you do so.

Now turn our attention to your hands and arms. Take the identical three breaths in for each section, moving in turn from your finger tips to your elbows and then your elbows to your shoulders. Next connect up the energy from your shoulders to your throat, which you have reached before, with the same technique. You can now take the breath and the energy from your throat to your forehead and lastly from here to the top of your head.

Do be sure that the energy you create does not move out above the top of your head. You will have already connected here and the object of this meditation is to generate more energy for yourself, not to be sent out. Simply ensure that your focus is on the area within your head, not outside of it. Before you finish take a moment to be aware now of your state of being and your needs at this time, noticing any difference there may be.

From here you can return from your meditation, remembering to ground before you re-join the everyday world, open your eyes or stand up. Be careful to return but also do not make such a strong flow of force so that the energy you have created is given back to the Earth. Be sensitive and remember that energy exists on a subtle realm and level. As you deepen you're breathing on your return, just press your feet down on to the floor where you are a little and you should find this grounds you enough.

The technique for the Recharging Exercise is as follows:

Ground and Connect

Pause and consider you needs

Breathe gold from head to feet, seven breaths

Breathe silver from feet to head, seven breaths

Take three breaths in stages up through your body

Pause to reconsider your needs.

Ground

This technique will leave you refreshed and revitalised, from the tips of your toes to the top of your head. It will leave you glowing with health and vitality. Because of this it can be tempting to rush out and catch up on all the hundreds of tasks awaiting your attention. Do not fall into this trap! Instead take it easy and conserve that energy. You should find that you sleep soundly the next night, when your energy system will process the influx it has received and enable you to take the full benefit from this meditation. Should you follow the impulse to rush around, you would find yourself quickly drained and over tired and in a worse state than when you started. What is needed is simply for the energy to soak into you and the aforementioned 'energy system' to do its job.

In the next Chapter we will examine and explore how we can use this energy system for health of Body, Mind and Spirit and more besides, but before we do so, there is one more meditation we must master before we will know how to use the system that operates on the energy level in each of us.

Basic Colour Breathing

This meditation utilises two aspects of energy that we will meet in much greater detail later in the book. These are colour and the concept of the chakras, or energy centres. The primary purpose of introducing this exercise here is to deepen your awareness and sensitivity to energy.

In this meditation we divide the basic flow of life-force energy into its main colour components, which are the colours of the rainbow, the colour spectrum. As we shall see when we explore the human energy field in the next Chapter, these colours are each linked to a different level in the human being, via one of the chakras. For the purposes of this meditation this is all the knowledge that is required for its successful working.

The meditation is a good one to induce an overall healing, whilst also giving the option of a specific flow of healing energy to any one particular level or area. It is an excellent raining method for personal awareness, giving the practitioner a deep concept and sensation of the human system at a level that reaches deeper and beyond the physical.

Through this one gains an awareness of one's interaction with the wider world and Universe surrounding ourselves. This exercise is therefore a method of developing personal responsibility that stems from this increased awareness and capacity for interaction. These benefits are, remember, subtle, but no less powerful and significant for this.

To begin the Basic Colour Breathing, Ground and Connect yourself in the usual manner and become aware of that place of balance and peace within, that lies at the centre of all living things. Reflect on this for a time and consider what blocks or hindrances might be preventing you from experiencing a full awareness of this peace and stillness. This may be on any level (or combination thereof), whether spiritual, mental, emotional or physical. Do not react to this blockage, but simply become aware of it. There is no judgement, thought or feeling here, only awareness. Allow yourself to become aware of what is standing between you and a deep inner peace in your being and in your life. Do not search for answers, but allow them to come to you. The more you try, the harder it is.

When you are ready, let yourself be aware of your breathing. Notice from where you are breathing in your body and take your breath to a deep level down in your stomach. This ensures that you are able to relax, rather than breathing from your chest, which is a sign of strain. Slowly and easily establish a pattern and rhythm to your breathing, just a little deeper than is usual for you in meditation. The aim here is of course to remain at ease with your breath and keep relaxed, but being aware of your breathing so that a relaxed concentration is required to maintain that focus. This in itself generates a flow of energy through your breathing. Ensure that your breathing is unhurried and not forced in anyway and allow yourself to fall into this pattern of breathing as you continue the meditation.

When you feel ready to, bring your mind into a clear point of focus and attention and concentrate on the area at the base of your spine. This area is from the back of your body and out to the front. It exceeds your physical body by a few inches in front and behind. As you level your focus on this area of your body and being, begin to add the colour red to the feel and flow of your in-breath. Simply imagine that the air you are breathing in is red. This should be a medium and clear red, without marks of any kind, not too dark and not too light, which is a general principle of all the colours that you breathe in, in this meditation.

As you breathe in the colour red, imagine and try to sense the effect it has upon you, as it flows around the area of the base of your spine. Feel the energy of the red permeating your being and body at this level, energising you and lifting you. Breathe this red colour in for a total of seven breaths, but do not worry too much over the count. It is more important to have a good awareness and feel for the effect of the colour red that you draw in to yourself as you breathe. Breathe in for several breaths and the job will be done, drawing the red level of the spectrum in to yourself to relax for a few breaths.

Now move up a level, this time to your stomach and specifically to a point just below the navel. As you breathe in now, add the colour orange to your breath and draw this into your being, both in front and behind, as before, for seven breaths. Also as before, be aware of any feelings or sensations you may have that seem to result from the effects of the orange energy that flows into you now. This may be in the form of heat, cold, tingling, images, feelings, thoughts, symbols, worlds and so on. Do not react to them, but remain aware of the effect of each colour upon you as you breathe it in to yourself. Breathe in for the seven breaths then and let yourself relax for a moment as you adjust to moving up to the next level.

When you feel ready, bring the focus of your mind and concentration to the area of your solar plexus, the hollow just below the ribs. At this level through your body breathe in the clear and even colour of yellow, as before for seven breaths. Remain aware of its effect upon you, taking as long as you need for this process to occur. Let yourself rest for a few moments to acclimatise and adjust and then move on.

Now bring your focus to the level of your heart and here you breathe into and through your body the colour of green. This again should be neither too dark nor too light. Breathe this green energy and colour in for seven breaths, observing its apparent effect upon you and then rest once more.

Next move up to the level of your throat, the energy centre here being located at the base of the neck, where there is a soft area. The colour of the energy to breathe in here is blue, again neither dark nor light. See what effect the seven breaths in of this colour has upon your being and again rest before proceeding. This is important to adjust yourself and allow a chance for the energy to settle within you at the appropriate level.

Move up in your concentration to your forehead, again moving through the body front and back. This is the area of the (in) famous Third Eye, a very sensitive area. Here breathe in an indigo colour. Indigo is a combination of blue and violet, resulting in what is often called purple, but be sure the colour you visualise is not too dark. Here you may begin to sense more responses as this level is very sensitive and connected to higher matters. Be gentle and do not force anything, simply breathe in in seven indigo breaths in the same manner as before.

Rest when you have completed the breaths and move up to the last level in this meditation. This is the crown level, situated just on top and in the centre of your head. Here you breathe in a violet colour, still purple but much lighter than before. Again this is connected to higher stimulus and awareness and you may pick up quite strong sensations. If you do not, do not worry, the object of this meditation is not to discover clairvoyant information, but to develop your awareness of the being you truly are and so gain greater control over yourself. Breathe in seven violet breaths and then rest.

Now you have moved up through the levels and energy centres of your body, finishing at the highest level. This may leave you feeling as if you have grown enormously or that your head has expanded in all directions. These and other similar sensations are just awareness of the energy.

You may feel light headed and distant from the outside world. Just accept these sensations as you will soon become accustomed to them and they are not harmful – in fact usually very pleasant and valuable as a tangible means of knowing something is happening.

Remain where you are for a few moments, for however long feels comfortable for you. Do not lose your focus and begin to think with your everyday mind however. If this begins to happen, it is time to return. Whilst you are there, consider now what there is to prevent you from feeling the deep peace and balance at the heart and centre of your being.

At this level, there should be very little if anything. Certainly this meditation takes you above the seemingly important troubles of our linear world. Here you come to a more true and accurate perception of things as they truly are. Let yourself take this in and when you are ready, make your return.

From this high level it is vital that you do return and the sensations you may be feeling now demonstrate precisely why you must ground before you get up. To do this, focus again on your physical body and on your feet. Imagine everything within your body flowing down and returning to its usual form. Feel your feet and your body on the floor you are on and press your feet down a little. Gradually and slowly increase the depth of your breathing until it is back to normal. When you are ready, let your eyes open and take time to adjust before you move.

The technique for Basic Colour Breathing is:

Ground and Connect
Pause to consider blocks to peace
Breathe in red to the base of the spine
Breathe in orange to the stomach
Breathe in yellow to the solar plexus
Breathe in green to the heart
Breathe in blue to the throat
Breathe in indigo to the forehead
Breathe in violet to the crown
Pause to consider your peace
Ground

This exercise gives you a taste of what can be achieved through meditation and is excellent for increasing your perception of things. This reminds me of a technique suggested to me long ago and still used today, when one feels surrounded and surmounted by problems and troubles. Imagine that you rise up so that you look down on the room or space that you are in. Then move up further and look down on the house or building you are in, then the street, then the town and on up until you can see the whole area. Keep right on going until the country is in view and then the whole of the globe of Earth. Drift on out to space and then remember your overwhelming problems. Sometimes they are not quite so important out here. Return back down to your body where you are and consider your troubles again – it is usually much easier!

The Basic Colour Breathing Meditation does the same as the above, but within the parameters of your own body and being. This leads us nicely on to the next area of meditating with energy that we must explore in this way – that of the energy system of the human.

Chapter 5 – Energy System Meditations

We have so far seen and sensed the life force energy that flows through all living things, whether it be animal, plant or human. We have explored and experienced how this energy can be utilised to help us gain more awareness and so control over ourselves and our lives. Central to this has been the idea of placing our consciousness at the very heart of our beings, from where our sense of peace stems. By accessing this place of peace we have been able to bring this fully into our everyday lives.

Now the time has come to explore the working of this process, examining how we absorb this life force energy into ourselves and how it is converted into emotions and actions. Through this we come to see how we can utilise this process to establish what we require in the daily reality we experience.

Through this book I have referred variously to the body and the being. These are distinct, yet linked. The body is the physical and readily tangible, skeleton and skin and all that lies between. The being is taken as referring to the physical body, with the addition of the energy system that surrounds it. This is most commonly known as the aura or human energy field that surrounds and permeates that physical body. We must look at this in a little more detail however and introduce the relationship between the aura, the chakras, and the glands and thus some inner workings of the body.

The aura is an electromagnetic field emanating from the physical body in normal, healthy adults up to about two to three feet from the physical body. It contains a great deal of information and can sometimes be seen by those with a good degree of inner perception. This is usually in the form of colours, which we have already looked at to some degree in the basic Colour Breathing Meditation. The aura is constantly absorbing life force energy from all around, in the sunlight, from the air, from other living beings and so on. It is the condition and quality of this energy that goes a long way to shaping who and what we are. It therefore follows that we can tap into that flow and make use of it in a beneficial way.

The aura has within it several levels which each contribute an aspect of our complete identity. We shall explore these aspects when we perform the Aura Meditations. Once absorbed into the aura this energy, from which all life stems, flows into the chakras, from where it is able to move into the physical system. Chakra is a Sanskrit word meaning wheel or disk and each chakra can be viewed as an energy vortex or power centre, with a concentrated flow of life force moving through it.

There are seven main chakras located at the points on the spine and above, which we focussed on in basic Colour Breathing, but there are many more minor chakra points on the palms, feet, and knees and so on. Here we are concerned only with the seven main and familiar chakras. Each chakra absorbs and processes energy from the aura that relates to an aspect and specific level of our being. A good and healthy flow through each chakra is necessary for good health at each of these levels and in combination. Through the Chakra Meditations included here we shall see how we can maintain this flow and so maintain good health, and more besides.

It is clear then that the energy systems of the human being play a vital and major role, underpinning ad shaping that which is experienced physically, whether as symptoms of illness, feelings, thoughts or actions. At this energy level we can pre-empt these things and so construct the physical reality that we wish for ourselves. We must first be reminded here how important it is to be fully accepting of the idea that all things happen first at this energy level.

This concept must be absorbed into your consciousness before you will be able to use the meditations in this Chapter to their full effect. Recall the maxim that 'energy follows thought' and you have the reason for this. The more focussed your thoughts and concentration, the better the energy that flows from them. Any doubts or wanderings affect the flow of energy, which as we see affects the reality you experience. It would not do to have a world that faded in and out occasionally because we could not concentrate due to doubts that it was actually there!

Aura Awareness

This meditation is a good technique for making yourself aware of the existence of the aura if you do have doubts. More effectively this meditation can be used for preventative medicine, helping to prevent physical dis-ease from occurring, by maintaining the condition of the aura. Just like the physical body, the aura benefits from movement and fluidity and it is this which this meditation provides for the aura. In essence we have here a workout for the aura – the first new-age workout!

This meditation is one perhaps best performed lying down. If you choose to do this, make sure that your head is supported by a small cushion or pillow. If necessary here, re-read the section on posture in Chapter One to find out the best position for you. This meditation is also one of the rare occasions where grounding and connecting is not necessary. This is because you are not 'going within' in the meditation or journeying anywhere. Indeed, grounding strongly may hamper awareness in this exercise, as we are attempting to move into the aura a little. It is however, very necessary to ground afterwards as usual.

To begin, close your eyes and let your body relax. As you lie there, allow your body to spread out on the floor as you relax more and more. Take a good deep breath, holding on to this for a moment before letting it go and relaxing as you breathe out.

Imagine and feel that your body slithers out over the floor, letting all tension go. Let the floor take your weight fully. Let go of your breathing and allow this to happen in its own natural way, without strain or effort in any way.

Be aware then of the limits of your physical body. Just lie there and sense where your body ends, mentally travelling all around the outline of your body. Begin at your feet, move up one side (it does not matter which), move over your head and back down the other side to your feet again. Move slowly and steadily, keeping your focus and concentration. Take as long as you need and do not rush. It is better to go too slow than too fast. When you are back at your feet, you now have a good awareness of your physical body and its area of being.

Now let your body become weightless. Do this by bringing to mind the fact that your body is formed primarily of energy. Sense and feel your own life force energy within you. Feel its flow and movement over your body. As you are relaxed it is easy to feel that you are very light. Imagine yourself becoming lighter and lighter with each breath you take and soon you are completely weightless, imagining that you are floating just a little off the floor.

In your imagination now, let your body stretch itself, first above your head and then below your feet, by a distance of only about two inches. This is not that you become taller, but that you actually drift up by three inches and then down by three inches. Sense your response to this and feel how it feels. The object here is to move into your aura, above then below.

When you have done this, return again to your physical body as it floats above the floor, motionless and weightless. When you are ready, pausing for as long as you need, imagine that you move up once more, this time to a distance of about a foot. Sense how this feels and then move back through your body, then below it to a distance of about a foot once more.

Again, note your response and feeling here.

Pause if you wish and then continue. This time move up above your physical body to the edge of your aura, a distance of approximately two to three feet. Move slowly and gently and take your time. Let yourself move up and sense what you may. Then move below to the edge of your aura and sense what you may here.

It is important now to move back to your physical body for the next stage of this meditation. Now we begin to expand and contract the aura itself. This can give rise to some quite powerful and strong feelings and responses so do proceed gently and cautiously. When you are ready, turn your attention to your breathing, but only become aware of it, do not change or alter it in any way. Let your breath remain natural and easy.

As you breathe in, imagine and sense that you are drawing in the aura. Allow yourself to breathe out naturally and keep focussed on your in-breath, sucking in the aura all the while. Little by little the aura will contract until it will be quite tight over you. This may make you feel a little uncomfortable or at worst very slightly claustrophobic.

Be aware of your response to what you are doing and continue this part of the meditation until you feel that your aura is now close to your physical body. You may feel a little pressure upon you, as the energy of the aura moves in. Remain like this for a short time, floating above the floor still and aware of your aura close all around you. Feel it beneath your body as well as above and below and to the sides.

Now turn your attention to your out breath, again without altering the level of your breathing. As you focus on your exhalation, allow your aura to move out. Continue to concentrate on your out breath and on allowing your aura to expand out, beyond its usual size to the very edges it can go to. As you do this, you will begin to feel a sense of expansion and space that is very pleasant and also allows for a good sense of your capabilities.

Breathe the aura out and expand it for as long as seems necessary and then take a moment to pause and collect your senses, feeling what you can and letting sensations and awareness come to you. Relax and drift now if you wish.

Having taken as long as you need, begin then to make your return. Return your awareness to your physical body and become aware of its weight once more. By doing this you will return yourself fully to your physical body. Make yourself aware of its weight and of yourself lying on the floor once more. From here ground in the usual manner, taking your time as is usual and necessary.

The technique for Aura Awareness is as follows:

Lie down, relax the body
Move upwards and then downwards three inches
Move upwards then downwards one foot
Move upwards then downwards two – three feet
Move back to the physical body
Breathe the aura in
Breathe the aura out
Ground

This meditation is an excellent preliminary to the techniques that follow. It is also of great practical use if you want to get yourself noticed, or alternatively remain unnoticed! Simply breathe the aura in if you do not wish to be revealed or breathe it out if you want to attract attention.

Aura Meditations

The aura has been studied and commented upon for thousands of years, more recently much attention being given to its structure and use in the field of healing. Healers and now some scientists have found that the transmissions of life force energy into appropriate parts of the aura has a beneficial effect in aiding a patient's recovery.

What actually happens is that the influx of energy facilitated by the healer allows for the patient to heal themselves. Exactly where this energy should be directed within the aura depends on the location and nature of the dis-ease affecting the patient. This will also depend on one's method of breaking down the aura for this purpose.

It is widely accepted that there are seven main bodies or layers to the aura, existing beyond the physical body. Each permeates the physical body and overlaps the previous one, extending out beyond until the last or seventh layer reaches out to two or three feet from the physical. Each of these seven layers relates to one of the chakras located along the spine, linking the innermost, 'etheric' layer of the aura with the physical body. Thus, each chakra draws life force energy in from the level of the aura to which it is aligned. In the chakra meditations that follow we look at the relevance of these seven layers and learn to utilise each aspect as it contributes to our wholeness.

For the aura meditations now, we must use the other accepted way of dividing the aura. This is into four 'bodies' or areas, each having its own specific function. It is to these functions that we turn now in our aura meditations.

The four bodies of the aura are then the etheric, emotional, mental and spiritual, each relating to that area of ourselves and our lives. The spiritual relates to inspiration, spiritual awareness and feeling and so on. The mental body relates to the workings of the mind and psychological condition. The emotional relates to feelings and emotions in our lives. The etheric (from 'ether' and relating to that which is between matter and energy, form and force) relates to the more mundane aspects, the instincts we each have that we respond to at this level. The etheric is looked upon as the energy equivalent or counterpart of the physical body.

It should be mentioned at this stage that I have not gone into detail regarding the structure of the aura, their relationships to the chakras and the way in which our lives are determined from this level. This is not at the expense of accuracy, but so that you can learn the basics of how this energy system works. Once this is grasped you have all you need for successful meditation. My aim is not to impress with how complex these things are, for they are not. Rather, I would like to enable you to sense these energies for yourself through meditation and to be able to use them to create and live in a manner more befitting a cosmic creature with enormous potential. Only then will we be able to take full responsibility for ourselves and the Universe in which we live and which, by this energy system, we are an intrinsic part of. Those wishing to learn in more detail the workings of this system, I would refer to the books *'Hands of Light'* and *'Light Emerging'* (see Bibliography).

Etheric Energy Body Meditations

To begin, ground and connect yourself in the usual way and come to the place of balance at the centre of your being. From here extend your inner, subtle senses out and allow yourself to become sensitive to the existence of energy. Allow yourself, (not try), to feel the movement and flow of your etheric energy through and over your body, extending out no more than two or three inches from you. Let images and feelings come to you, as you explore this etheric realm with your mind and senses.

The etheric energy layer is often perceived as a bluish hue of colour, looking like sparks of blue light moving along the energy lines of the body and this first layer of the aura. See what you may perceive of this, but again, do not try too hard. Be aware also of any of the 'energy sensations' you may feel. This can be the usual tingling, heat, cold, or other similar sensations. This is the response you notice to the movement of the etheric energy, as compelled by your thoughts and mind, not the energy itself.

Allow yourself sufficient time to become aware of the etheric layer, which attunes your mind and yourself to its frequency, or its speed of movement. A brighter or bluer hue to the colour you may perceive indicates a quicker frequency, which can mean increased thought patterns, a stressed, troubled or over-active mind and a certain nervousness and anxiety in the individual. A darker or greyer hue to the colour can indicate a slower thinking, more contemplative mind, which could also be a little sluggish or depressed. The etheric energy can best be sensed by seeking it out with your senses since it is through these that you experience it. Try to feel a pulsing through your body that extends out over you. Imagine your body having a grid of energy lines over and through it.

Become aware now that it is from this etheric energy level and layer that your body, mind, actions and reality are formed. With your mind you can thus influence this reality at all these levels. You can therefore improve the quality of your own reality by creating not a faster flow of etheric energy, but a better quality one. Through that grid of energy lines imagine that a white light shines. See and sense this as a series of white lines running over and through your body. Feel the white light acting as a cleansing agent for your etheric layer. Be gentle with this as some powerful sensations can sometimes result. Continue this action until you feel that the white light has moved through the whole of your body.

We relate to the etheric energy, or rather it relates to us, through the medium of our senses, those of touch, sight, sound, smell, taste and intuition. This constitutes the next stage of this meditation. Consider what brings you physical pleasure and ask yourself if you are allowing yourself enough time for this in your life. What physical needs might you be neglecting at this time and how can you redress this? Resolve to take whatever action is necessary.

Consider your surroundings now. These are not the walls or space around you as you meditate but your everyday environment Do you take notice of this and appreciate it? Is it beautiful to you or Ugly? What and why is it ugly or beautiful? Do you consider the colour and décor or where you live and how might you improve this to better suit you as an individual? How might you make your surroundings cleaner or less polluted?

Now move on to consider what you hear on a daily basis as you live your life. Do you take notice of the sounds around you or do you live in a world inside your head, so your thoughts blot out outside noise? Are you easily distracted by noise? Is there a great deal of man-made noise about you or can you hear the sounds of nature on a daily basis? Do you listen to music or hear the chatter of television for many hours of the day? What effect do all these things have upon you and how might you improve this aspect of your life?

Move on in your thoughts to the use of fragrance and smell in your life. What smells do you encounter regularly and how do these affect you? Do you perfume yourself and your home and for what purpose and effect? Are you aware of unnatural smells that might adversely affect you in your life and how might you take steps to eliminate these and their detrimental effect upon you?

Now consider the effect of taste in your life. Do you really stop to taste your food and how does this affect you? Do you enjoy the taste of food or do you feel that your taste buds are overridden by chemical in your food, tobacco or excessive alcohol? How might you improve this aspect of your being?

Lastly consider your intuition. Do you have a feel for what this is and how you relate to it? What forms does your intuitive awareness take and do you respond to it or ignore it? Do you pause long enough to listen to what your instincts are telling you in your life or rush headlong into the next experience? How might you allow your intuition to guide you more and be closer to its guidance?

When you have considered these aspects of your life to your satisfaction, make your return fully and gently, by returning your awareness to your breath and your body and grounding in the usual way.

The objective here is not a hedonistic experience of the senses but simply taking time out to be aware of how your senses are affecting you, as this is all too infrequent in our rushed and busy lives these days. On a deeper level you become more aware of each of your senses in the altered state of consciousness that meditation brings and so at this level you are able to make changes, in your mind, that have their outworking and result in your everyday life. This is therefore an excellent meditation and method for improving the quality of one's life.

Emotional Body Meditation

Every emotion we feel has a corresponding movement of energy in the aura. We often relate our feelings and emotions to colours, as in 'feeling blue', 'seeing red' and so on. This is reflected in the movement of colour in the aura, via our emotions. A 'blob' of colour is released, or projected each time we have a feeling. As an example to illustrate this, when a person is attracted to another, a pink colour is projected towards them. If the two are compatible, the same is returned and off we go! If not the colour is absorbed back into the sender, or rejected. How conditioned we are as regards rejection depends on how we react to the feeling of this pink energy being returned to us. This is one small example in a myriad of energy workings through our emotions.

Begin this meditation with your grounding and connecting. Come to that centre of yourself and feel the security here, from where you can safely regard your emotions and feelings, without judgment and reaction. Once relaxed and 'centred' allow yourself to consider what emotions are prevalent in you and your life at this time. Do not react to these but simply become aware of them. Consider how they are affecting you and your actions in life. Think also of how satisfied you are with your feelings. Do they trouble you, and are you comfortable with them? Consider if you would wish to feel more or less in life. Are you comfortable with others' displays of emotion around you or does this make you wish they weren't?

Realise now that you are in a position to shape your feelings and the effect of your emotions upon you from this meditative state. Take a moment or two to make yourself fully aware of this, for clarity of mind is all important here. The highest state of emotion is regarded as unconditional love, whether for oneself, others, the Earth or the Universe. Imagine and see a pink hue flooding gently over your body and extending out beyond you, to a distance of six inches or so (the exact distance does not matter). Open yourself and your emotions to receiving this feeling of unconditional love. If you feel nothing this means that you are blocking the feeling at some level. Consider why this may be so and how you may be preventing yourself from receiving unconditional love. Let the pink flood through your being and saturate you. Be aware of your response to this and how it makes you feel.

Take as long as you need or wish with this section of the meditation. When you are ready to, consider again your emotions as outlined above. Ask yourself the same questions as before, seeing if there is a difference in your feeling now. Again be aware not to react or judge. Be gentle with yourself, and honest. When you have concluded your wanderings, let yourself return, grounding in the usual way. Take a moment or two before you move as this meditation can yield some surprisingly powerful feelings and responses. Unconditional love can leave us feeling light headed as it is really a very high and powerful source of energy that shapes our Universe – or would if we would let it.

Mental Body Meditation

With this meditation we turn our attention to that which is one of the strongest underlying energies that go to make us who and what we are, that of habitual thought. The mental body is usually coloured yellow and seen strongest about the head and shoulders for obvious reasons. The bright or dullness of the yellow depends on the type of thoughts we have – happy or sad, to simplify things. The overall yellow colour is tainted by blobs of other colours, which are associated with the emotions we have. Thus if an idea or thought – is well formed and clear so will the corresponding colour be in our aura. Habitual thoughts become solidified within the aura, as they crystallise. It is for this reason that habits are hard to break. It is also for this reason that through meditation, they are easy to break!

This is because meditation can bring about a change of consciousness or awareness and it is from this level that our everyday selves and lives come. At the deeper or higher level of meditation we are at a level of creativity and inspiration. What we determine in our minds or resolve whilst in meditation is therefore very powerful. We can see then how we can use meditation to help break addictive behaviour or thought patterns. You cannot overdose on meditation, so perform this daily if you wish to give up smoking, drinking, gambling etc. You will also gain a much greater overall control of your mind and its effect upon you through this meditation.

Begin with your grounding and connecting and find your centre. Let your senses stretch out and imagine your mental body extending out to about eight inches from your body. Imagine this is a yellow colour. What type of yellow comes naturally to mind – is it dark or light and what does this tell you about your current state of mind?

Now consider how your mind is affecting you and your life at this time. Do you have a constant chatter of endless thoughts running through your mind and do you wish it would stop? How might you do this? Do you rely solely on your mind and not your emotions to make your decisions? Do you wish your mind was different, more relaxed, happier, and more positive? How can you make it more as you would wish?

Consider if you have any habitual thoughts, whether recent or old and established and on any level. Consider here if there are habits you wish to break in your life, or form. Resolve in your mind to do so, having become clear as to your reasons why. Now see a clear, bright flow of yellow flood your being and body. Let this move out over and through you. Feel it clearing your mind and head as it foes. See and sense the effect this has upon you. Let old, outmoded ways of thinking and behaving that you wish to leave behind flow away from you and dissolve to nothing. Continue this process until you feel that you have achieved a new clarity of mind.

Now consider once more your state of mind and its effect upon you. See what difference you sense within now. Ask yourself the questions above once more and note how you feel and react mentally to these now. Spend time being aware of the new awareness in your mind and when you are ready make your return, grounding in the usual manner.

Spirit Body Meditation

The spiritual body or layer of the aura does not have such a definite shade of colour as the other bodies, being made up really of all the colours. It is often perceived as a shimmering of colours. This is because its vibration – the speed of movement of the colours and energies – is much quicker than those of the 'lower' bodies. Often the colours perceived are gold and silver. These colours are usually looked upon as being the masculine and feminine colours respectively, each human being a combination of these two, being perhaps the dual aspects of the Divine, but this depends on your view of what or who 'God/dess' is.

It is at this highest level of our individual perception that our identities and 'destinies' are made and planned. When we access this level through meditation our attention then turns towards the subject of our overall lives and level of fulfilment in those lives. Much can be done here to shape and distil the essence of ourselves into a more focussed, coherent form. When our energies are viewed in this format, then we are more direct, more focussed in the daily reality of our lives.

Begin this meditation with your grounding and connecting as usual and allow your senses to extend out from your centre to encompass the whole of your being. It is important here to gain a good and clear awareness of the extent of your being, in its totality, as this is what the spiritual body represents. Let your inner senses be fully awake and alert, while your body is at rest and relaxed. Feel your whole being, reaching out to three feet or so from your physical body. Let yourself experience this and see how it feels to be aware of your complete self, perhaps for the first time.

Now consider the nature of your life and yourself at this time. Ask yourself how satisfied you are with your life. What might you do to improve this satisfaction? Do you feel fulfilled, not just in the usual sense of everyday things and materiality, but on a deeper level and with a spiritual element to this? Consider what your own spirituality is, and if you consider this to be in existence at all. Allow an awareness to your own spirituality to come to you and experience what this means to you. Consider how your spiritual awareness and self has relevance to your everyday life and how you might increase this, if you feel the need. Let your mind consider these subjects for as long as you feel you need. Do not force questions or answers in your mind but simply let them come to you.

Now let these thoughts go and instead turn your attention to the aura once more. Imagine a flow of gold and silver colour shimmering throughout your entire being. Let both colours flow equally over and within your body and aura. Be aware of any responses and stimulus you may have from this. Focus your mind on this flow of gold and silver colour and energy through your being, noting the response you have as it goes.

Now bring your mind back to the questions and thoughts given above and ponder these once more, seeing what difference the higher colours and energy of gold and silver may have made. Here you can programme you self at the highest level of creativity and can therefore align yourself fully with your destiny (if you view such things exist!) and certainly with full responsibility for your own being and life. Take as long as you need to allow your mind to wander over these subjects and then make your return, slowly and gently, ensuring that you're grounding is complete and that you return with your new awareness and realisations intact. Adjust completely before moving.

The structure of the Aura Meditations is a little different for each one, but for ease are summarised as follows:

Ground and connect
Become aware of aura body
Allow senses from this body to come to mind
Generate flow of colour energy to your being
Reconsider senses from this body
Ground

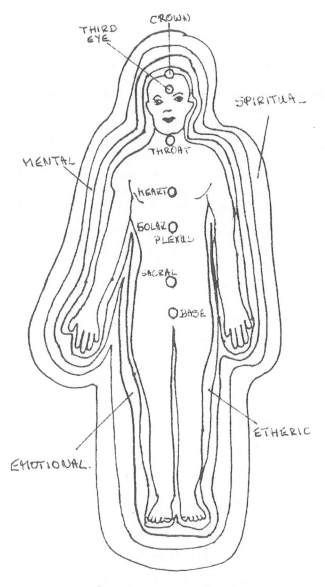

THE ENERGY SYSTEM

Chakra Meditations

We come now to a series of seven meditations, one for each of the seven main 'energy centres' of the body. Again there is a great deal of information regarding the chakras available, that I do not propose repeating here. Basic details have been given previously in this Chapter, being all that is required for these meditations.

There are a great many Chakras about the human body and aura, but we are only concerned with the seven predominant ones. As previously mentioned each of these chakras draws in life force energy from a particular body or level of the aura and adapts that energy into a form that can be used in the body. This is done primarily through the glands that are associated with each of the chakras. Please see the illustration for a description of these and their position on the body, together with the bodies of the aura.

We can see from the above that we draw not only our vital energy through the chakras, but also those substances into the body that predetermine our feelings and behaviour. These meditations allow us to tap into that process in a direct way and so are a very powerful way of creating the reality we want and need. We are able to draw in that which is relevant to us at any given time, focus it and release it into our lives. We are then in the optimum position to achieve what we want, how we want it. So meditation becomes eminently practical.

Each of the chakra meditations that follow involves opening the chakra in question. This permits an increased influx of energy which can create some strong sensations and resultant realisations. Care should therefore be taken, being as gentle with yourself as possible, as should be the case with all meditations, regardless of its content. The chakra meditations are subjective to your state of being at the time they are performed so can be performed whenever you wish.

For each of these meditations the structure is the same. This is given in the usual way at their end. The complete detailed structure is therefore given for the first, Base chakra meditation below and the necessary detail for each other meditation and chakra beneath this. Though you will have examined how you relate to your senses in the etheric body aura meditation, they are here examined individually and therefore in greater detail. Since we derive so much information from these senses this seems valid.

Base Chakra Meditation

This chakra is located at the base of the spine, where once our tail would have begun! The condition of this chakra indicates to a strong degree if you are sufficiently grounded in reality. Other details regarding this chakra are included in the following meditation description.

Begin with your grounding and connecting as usual. Now locate your attention on the area around the base of your spine. Spend a moment focussing on this. Become aware of any sensations you notice or that result from this. Now imagine that a closed flower is located at the base of your spine, facing forwards. See and feel that flower within your being and body. Now see the petals of the flower unfold and open. As it does so a red light shines out from the flower, around this area of your body and being. Be aware of how this feels as it happens ad what you notice as a result. Continue to visualise the flower unfolding until all the petals are completely open. This will open the chakra for you. This allows for the necessary energy to flow into you through this chakra.

Often we are depleted or 'leaking' energy, for many and varied reasons. Opening each chakra in these meditations allows for a replenishment of our vital energy, vital not only in nature but in necessity for our well-being. Spend as long as you feel you need to visualise and absorb a flow of red energy into this chakra, or flower. Note the response you have and how this makes you feel. The colour should be clear and of a medium hue in the range, as it should for each of the chakra colours, given below.

You may like to use the method of breathing in the red (or appropriate colour) to the chakra, rather than through the flower, if this is more comfortable to you. In this case, each time you inhale, without changing your breathing at all, feel the red colour and energy moving through your body and down to, in this case, the base chakra.

Breathing the red colour energy in will increase your basic life force, for we draw earth energy up into our beings through this chakra, vital to our sense of identity and to our feeling of security about who we are and our presence in the world. Whilst you draw in the colour then, feel the inner strength and commitment returning to you, energising the very essence of your being. Now let that red flow cease and just exist in the space you now find yourself.

This chakra is aligned to the spinal column and to your bones in general so be aware of any sensations you may feel in your skeletal structure. Spend a little time now considering how 'real' you feel, how attached to your body you are and your dependence upon it. These may sound strange things to be thinking about, but it is often precisely that which we take for granted that is in need of attention. So, give your attention to these things now. Notice what your intuitive mind tells you and allow your inner senses to guide you. Spend as long as you wish on this.

When you are ready, turn your attention to your sense of smell, which the Base chakra is linked to. Breathe in through your nose for a time and see what effect this has upon you. Consider if you notice the scents and fragrances that come to you in the course of your day and how you respond to them. What can you smell now and what effect does it have upon you? Smell is one of the most powerful senses and can evoke strong memories. Think about what smells you recall from certain places and times in your life. Be aware of your use of smell and consider how you might make more use and greater awareness and pleasure of this in your life. You may surprise yourself with what you encounter here as these can often be unconscious memories. Allow scenes, images, places and associated feelings to drift up to you, noting anything unfamiliar for research later. Remember, be gentle. You can communicate with this deep part of your mind and self as if you were holding a conversation with an old and trusted friend, so address it in your head in this manner and sense the answers in your head also. You will always receive the truth.

If you have any problems with blood, with depression or with fear or excessive worry then you might like now to visualise a flow of red colour energy to the relevant area. This might be your head for worries or fear, your feet if you are feeling sluggish and excessively tired or run down, to generate energy into your system. If you feel in need of grounding in general, you could send red colour and energy down into the earth from the base of your spine. (This is also an effective earthing method at the end of any meditation, you may wish to try.) If you have any kidney problems, visualise a strong flow of red energy to your kidneys and to this chakra in general as this will strengthen them.

Lastly here, we can often release suppressed emotions by opening this chakra. Turn your mind to anything you may be holding back and need to let go of and be released from. Allow feelings and emotions from deep within you to well up to the surface. Consider why you may have suppressed this feeling and what you might do about it now. Is there any action that is necessary on your part to help you be free of it? What effect is it having upon you and your life? Take this aspect of the meditation as far as you wish, in your own way and to what conclusion you wish. Remember that you are in control and that this is a safe and supportive way for you to release your own repressed emotions and to release them in an entirely beneficial way.

Spend as long as you wish on this and when you feel ready close the chakra. This is vital to do, for if left open your energy would soon deplete and leave you run down, tired and vulnerable to any infections around you. To close the chakra, visualise the red colour receding back into the flower and then close the flower petals tightly shut once more. This is absolutely vital. When this has been done, ground yourself and return.

Sacral Chakra Meditation

The Sacral Chakra is located just below the navel. Remember that these energy centres exist and work through the body at their position.

To begin this meditation, perform your grounding and connecting as usual and then focus your concentration on the location of the sacral chakra. Become conscious of any sensations or feelings that come to you as you begin to feel this energy centre. Now imagine the flower located here and visualise and sense its petals opening as with the base chakra meditation. Open this fully and begin your exploration of this chakra.

The colour of this area and level is orange so begin to breathe in a medium and clear orange colour. You may also like to see the orange colour emanating from within the flower you have just opened. See what effect this has upon you.

Consider now what it is you may be carrying with you that is part of your being and that you may have acquired, without consideration or request, but has become part of you. What effect may these things be having upon you and how might you rid yourself of these if you wish to? Let yourself sense whatever unconscious baggage you may be carrying and its effect upon your being and life.

Take a brief pause and now focus your thoughts on your sexuality. Consider what this means to you and how you feel you express your sexuality. Is this a force under your control and are you content with this? Perhaps you feel it is wild and free and should remain so.

Often we have guilt associated with out sexuality so consider if this applies to you and ask yourself what you are guilty of. Consider the masculine and feminine sexual nature and ask yourself if you are aware of these forces within you. How might you make yourself more aware of these polarities within your being?

This chakra is linked to our sense of taste so consider this aspect of your being. Do you take notice of your sense of taste or do you take this for granted? Consider all aspects of your sense of taste and how this affects you.

As this chakra is linked to our sexual nature, so it is concerned with the reproductive system in the body. If you have cause for concern here, focus on the orange colour becoming especially strong and clear around this area, to strengthen and help it.

Be aware of the space you now find yourself in and simply remain there for as long as you wish, allowing sensations, thoughts and realisations to come to you. When you are ready to make your return, close the flower at the sacral chakra as before, ensuring the petals are tightly shut, then ground yourself and open your eyes.

Solar Plexus Chakra Meditation

The solar plexus chakra is situated below the bottom of the rib cage and is often looked upon as the seat of the centre of the body. This very sensitive energy centre is the point from which the much quoted 'silver cord' attaches itself, when we dream or otherwise leave the body.

Begin with your grounding and connecting and then open the flower at this position, unfolding its petals to see a clear and balanced yellow colour emerging from within. Feel this around the appropriate area of your body and breathe the yellow light and energy for a short time. Be aware of the effect this is having upon you as you do so.

Now consider what it is that you need or wish to create in your life at this time. This can be done on any level and be as practical or spiritual as you wish. Consider why you wish to create this thing, whether tangible or not and for what purpose. What is your motivation here and who will your creation serve? Will this assist you in your development and quest through life? Be honest and allow your inner or higher mind to guide you, letting thoughts come to you as you meditate. Concentrate your mind then on what you wish to create, if you are sure you wish it. Allow the principle of 'energy follows thought' to do its work, letting the impulses flood through your brain from your concentration that will give you the ability and drive necessary to bring this to manifestation and reality.

Let yourself pause and rest for a moment and then focus on that which you wish to destroy from your life or that which is no longer needed. Consider the reasons for this, in a similar way to the above, realising why you have this desire. Consider if there is anything you hold onto that is destructive and should itself be destroyed from your being and life. Again focus on letting this go, again using the same all important principle of 'energy follows thought'.

This chakra is linked to the sense of sight so consider now your ability to see in your life. Do you really notice what is around you or do you walk everywhere with your head down? Do you allow yourself you see reality and truth as it really is or do you look through rose tinted lens at everything? How might you see more clearly?

Physically, this chakra is linked to the internal organs such as the stomach, liver, spleen and gall bladder. If you have any problems in this area focus on the yellow colour for this chakra and this will strengthen things to give your natural healing process a boost.

Let yourself consider these subjects and their relevance to your life for as long as you wish and then make your return. See the yellow recede back into the flower and close the petals tightly. Ground yourself and return when you are ready to do so.

Heart Chakra Meditation

This chakra is not surprisingly located at the level of the heart and is therefore linked to all matters to do with the heart, both emotional and physical.

Begin as usual and open the flower of this chakra with a green colour and energy. This is the colour of balance and healing so this will leave you centred and aware of the truth of yourself and with a wonderful healing glow about you. Pause and adjust to this awareness.

Now consider the nature of love and its presence in your life. Do you love yourself? This simple question can bring up so many opinions, reactions and feelings, so let yourself have plenty of time to consider how you feel about it. Be aware then that the highest form of love is unconditional love, a love that neither demands nor expects but is imply given, freely and abundantly. Is this force present in your being and life and how might you increase it? Are you able to feel this same love for those you dislike or are your enemies your competitors? How might you demonstrate this in your life?

Give yourself time to pause and rest and then continue. Now focus on your sense of touch, which this chakra relates to. Do you notice how often you touch others and how you react when they touch you? Think about how you are when you shake hands with someone, hug them or give a more intimate embrace. Do you dislike others touching you and why? What does your awareness of touch tell you about yourself?

Obviously heart problems can be helped with the green healing colour of this level, or surround the heart with a green colour, breathing it in and visualising this clearly in your mind. Problems with circulation and respiration can also be helped here.

Lastly in this meditation, which is perhaps a little simpler than the other chakras, being concerned chiefly with love, think about your ability to receive love. Any blockages you may have in this meditation are likely to be as a result of a lack of self-love, so spend a little time considering how you might learn to love yourself more. Allow thoughts and feelings to come to you and just spend time loving yourself.

When you are ready, close the flower of this chakra and sense the green light receding into it. Ground yourself and return with what you have learnt.

Throat Chakra Meditation

This chakra connects us to our ability to express ourselves, using the influence of the blue energy level. The subject and nature of truth is also relevant now.

Begin by opening the chakra flower by breathing in the blue energy and seeing the petals unfold to emit the light around the area at the base of the neck, where this energy centre is located. Let yourself be aware of the effect this has upon you and adjust to this level of consciousness.

Now begin to consider your self-expression. What is your primary form of self-expression and how do you use this? Do you speak the truth or do you have trouble being honest and clear? Do you say yes when you mean no? Are others troubled or offended by your communications?   Consider your appearance also as this is a powerful if unconscious form of self-expression. What do you think your appearance says to others and are you happy with this? How might you change things so as to be more truthful to the person within? How might you improve your self-expression so as to be more honest and clear, without causing offense or forgetting sensitivity?

Let yourself rest and pause from what can be a surprising area to consider, for a short time. The throat chakra is linked to our sense of hearing so turn your focus to this now. Consider what kind of sounds you hear in your daily life? Are they pleasant and productive or distractive and annoying to you? How might you place yourself in a better or quieter place? Do you hear what others are telling you clearly or do you perhaps hear only what you want to hear? How might you listen more clearly? Do you ever have real silence in your life?

This chakra is linked to our lungs, so when you have taken a suitable pause, breathe in the blue energy to your lungs if you feel you are in need of help in this area. This will also help with any difficulties you may have with your metabolism and the blue energy will help to calm things down.

Give yourself as much time as you need to consider the expressions of this chakra and when you are ready close it as usual and ground yourself. Pause to allow yourself to assimilate what you have realised and then open your eyes.

Third Eye Chakra Meditation

The third eye chakra is a sensitive area so do proceed carefully with this meditation. The colour linked here is indigo or purple. Here we turn our attention to intuition and awareness of our individuality.

Begin with breathing in the indigo colour energy to the area around your forehead, just above and between the physical eyes. Let the flower petals unfold here and be aware of any sensations you feel here, which can be quite intense, but not painful. You may notice a dull ache for a time afterwards if you have done very little meditation, but this will soon wear off when you have finished. (If it does not, you have not grounded properly, so enter meditation once more and make sure you do so!)

Now turn your focus to your intuitive sense. Consider if you listen to your intuition, your instinct or your conscience. These are all aspects of your intuition, which we all have. The question is whether we are still and quiet enough to listen to them and heed their guidance. They always guide us and give us truth and never mislead or let us down. Consider in what ways you use and listen to your inner voice and gut feelings and how you might improve this or take more notice of it.

This can be a vital process in our inner peace so ensure you give yourself as much time as you require to become clear on this aspect of your being.

Let yourself pause and drift for a moment and bring your mind back into focus. Consider now your inner self. This chakra is considered to be the seat of the soul by many and gives us our individual spark. Consider what it is that makes you the unique and individual being that you are. How aware of this are you in your everyday life and how might you become more so aware? This awareness is again vital to your progressing the way you should, from whatever viewpoint. From a clear vision here we create our lives to be the way we want them to be, so regaining our own power and cease living for others. Focus on this aspect of your being for as long as is required for it to become real to you and have its effect, then pause and rest a little once more.

In the physical body this chakra is linked to the nervous system. Focus on the indigo colour permeating your being to help any problems you may have here. You may also focus on the ears and nose as this chakra is also linked to these.

Remain in this meditation as long as you wish then return and ground in the usual way, closing the chakra and indigo colour before opening your eyes.

Crown Chakra Meditation

The Crown Chakra is the last and highest of the seven main energy centres of the body. It is located at the top and in the centre of the head, so as to receive the higher force of life we are now very used to. Its colour is violet or white if you prefer. It is linked to our spirituality amongst many other traits.

Begin with opening this chakra, possibly feeling yourself and your level of consciousness rising. Let this process happen, which can feel as if you are moving up and floating, and remain focussed on the chakra. Breathe in and absorb the violet or white colour and observe how this feels to you and its effect upon you.

When you are ready consider your spirituality. What does this mean to you and how do you give this expression in your life? Is this something you confine to meetings in appropriate places, when you feel like it or when it impresses others? Is it something that permeates the whole of your life, your being, body and its structure? Do you live, breathe, walk and talk your spirituality naturally, or is it forced in some way? Be honest here and afford yourself the opportunity to make progress. Let responses come to you and determine to act on them. How might your spirituality become more a part of your life and less something that is strange, ill-defined or abstract from your daily routine?

Give yourself a pause from these serious questions and continue when you are ready. Physically this chakra can help with your sense of creativity and inspiration, often seen as coming into the brain. Any problems with your head can be helped here, focussing on the white or violet light surrounding and seeping through your head.

Since the subject and nature of spirituality is a vital and large one, we confine this meditation to its exploration and to the resultant discoveries it brings. Our spirituality is something that is always evolving and moving on, just like our physical bodies. The only difference here is that our bodies die and decay, while our spirit lives on, so ultimately is more important. Consider how this is reflected in your life.

Pause long enough to allow yourself to assimilate all that you have considered and realised and make your return. This meditation can leave you a long way off from your daily life and it is vital that you come back to ordinary everyday reality fully and completely. Close this chakra in the usual manner and ground, slowly and clearly.

The technique for the chakra meditation is as follows:

Ground and connect
Open chakra
Visualise flower opening and breathing in colour
Reflect on and consider nature of chakra
Close Chakra, closing flower and absorbing colour
Ground

This completes our journey through the energy system of the human being, as it exists outside the physical body. There is a remaining energy system of the body that of the Meridians, which we will now take a brief look at.

Meridian Meditations

The existence of these energy systems of the human being have been known and accepted in the east far longer than the West. So it is that we look to Chinese medicine systems for this method of meditation that we can use for physical health, in both maintenance and improvement, the Chinese expounded the use of meridians within the body. These channels are vessels along which the same life force or energy that we are now familiar with flows. They are often viewed as also carrying the blood and body fluids round the body, but do not confuse them with the veins, arteries and capillaries.

116

The principles by which we work here are just the same as with the chakra system. To remind you, this is by the principle 'energy follows thought', the salient point here being that if we instigate a positive, pure and powerful flow of healing energy through our bodies, by the use of concentrated, focussed thought, this will be absorbed into your physical systems, thereby causing the same condition in our bodies in a tangible manner.

The Eastern view of energy or Chi permeating all things and existing in all things is one that we utilise here. As such in the meridian system there are concentrations of energy in certain places, dependent on the individual in terms of build, emotion, mental condition and much more besides, being that which makes the individual so. As such, blockages and weaknesses in this flow of energy through the body can be created by the disharmonious muscle movement, lingering emotion, and habitual negative thought and so on. By focussing a flow of pure energy force along the relevant meridian to clear the blockage or strengthen the weakness a return to health is instigated at the basic energy level.

The 'relevant meridian' is decided by its path and the organs and functions to which it is linked. As with the aura and chakra meditations, the method for each meridian meditation is the same, simply adjusting the route to fit the meridian being focussed on. These are given in the text for each individual meridian meditation, which are included for those that which to use them, in Appendix A. The outline for this meditation is then as follows:

Ground and connect
Become Aware of what you are treating, if anything specific
Visualise energy sphere along the path of the meridian line
Pause and take stock for realisation
Ground

The energy sphere that you visualise should be simply a clear and focussed ball of energy, not too bright not to dull and not of any particular colour. The objective to aim at is a pure, untainted

117

source of energy, the very stuff and source of life, nothing more and nothing less. Visualise and sense this and simply pass it through the meridian. If it has not faded away by the time you have finished, then pass it into the Earth. It may have collected and absorbed any negative energy you have been holding tonto and the Earth will deal with this in her usual magnificent manner!

During the meditations you may feel any of the previously described 'energy sensations', such as heat, cold, tingling etc. Remember that these are your responses to the energy, not the energy itself. What you sense and how you feel during the meditation may give you some idea as to the cause of a weakness or blockage in your system. The fact that you sense anything tells you that something is happening, it not being essential to understand what this is for to work. It will happen anyway, so long as you are able to keep your focus and concentration. Your level of concentration is in direct relation to the level, dose or quality of energy that you are able to transmit during the meditation, the benefit you obtain from it is likewise related. If you have followed the meditations in this book chronologically, practising faithfully as you went, your concentration should have reached a good level by now.

So we have the meridian system of energy vessels through the body along which we transmit a pure healing force, from start to end. This energy flow manifests as our physical condition, having its relation emotionally, mentally and spiritually, the human system being inter-related in this way. As such these meditations can be combined with complementary treatments such as acupuncture and reflexology. These treatments place needles or fingers at specific points to instigate the flow of energy along the meridians. Introducing a meditative concentration to the flow being treated at the same time significantly increases the effect. Be gentle with yourself however, for a uniform, balanced concentration of energy is what is required for healthy body mind and spirit, not a blazing volcanic lava flow! We now turn our attention to other ways in which meditation can be used for Healing.

Chapter 6 – Healing Meditations

I have mentioned earlier in the text how all meditations can be viewed as being 'healing', in the sense that every meditation you perform has some benefit for you. In the previous Chapter we looked at a specific kind of healing meditation and now we progress to a selection of meditations that are all specifically healing in nature and content, but that utilise different principles of the subject.

These meditations are presented in no particular order, each one in its known right being of some practical use in its field. It may perhaps be helpful to first define the state of health at which we are aiming by use of these meditations. This is best described as being a state of balance and equilibrium of Body, Mind and Spirit, giving a feeling and perception of overall well-being. Imbalances can be caused by many things, the result of which is often the various physical maladies that we, in our ignorance and limited perception, view as illness. These afflictions are best viewed as a last outworking of some state of dis-ease in our systems. As we have seen this means a great deal more than just the wondrous workings of our human bodies. This includes the energies of the human being and so we must look to the holistic health of Body, Mind and Spirit for our complete well-being.

Just as we share the Earth with all living things and as such are a part of them and they us, so must we come to realise that the recurrent headaches we feel, resulting from accumulated tension, are in turn the result of a deep seated fear or anxiety we have accrued, perhaps from childhood, or before. As such we must find a means of allowing ourselves to gently face those fears and perceived dangers lurking in our systems. The use of meditation, coupled with the appropriate remedy, is, I suggest, the most effective means of achieving this, whilst allowing the self to become the owner of an increased awareness, control and mastery over their being. In short, we become our own therapist, since no one knows ourselves better than we do. Let your inner or higher self be your guide and come walk with me through this wondrous field of meditation. Tread carefully however, for the jewels that lurk within are sharp and can cut, lest you treat them with disdain.

Seed Meditations

The first such technique we look at is best described as a general health inducing and promoting exercise, that is not only entirely beneficial to perform for any imbalance, dis-ease or illness you have identified or sense within your system, it also feels wonderful to do! The principles on which it is based are those of Nature.

As creatures of the Earth we share the same urges, senses and patterns as those which govern the life of this brilliant planet. Amongst others these are an urge to (pro) create, give life and increase, grow and develop. This is indeed, perhaps the essence of all life. This happens in all things, be it the Grand Canyon or the seed from which every blade of grass in your garden grows.

Since meditations on the Grand Canyon can be a little awesome (having been lucky enough to have experienced this) and assuming that not every reader of this book will have seen this sight, we will take the image of the seed as our focus. Quite simply, in this technique the objective is to align yourself with the growing procedure and practice of any seed, whether it be the tallest oak or the smallest, aforementioned, blade of grass.

This meditation is an excellent method of generating and improving one's vital energy and life force. It is good if you are feeling 'under the weather' (or for any condition that you may describe as 'under'!) since it lifts you up and above what is holding you down. At its best it can set you free and remind you of the freedom that exists in life itself and the simplicity of the warmth of the sunshine and the joy this can bring. The technique itself combines the use of healing energy, received from the Earth and the Universe, with visualisation.

The meditation itself is quite simple. Imagine that you are a seed. You are planted firmly into the ground and all around you there is warm, rich soil, full of nutrients and minerals, essential to your life and growth. You can breathe deeply and abundantly where you are. How you got there is a mystery that need not concern you at this stage, or indeed ever. For now it is enough to simply feel the warmth, safety and life around you. Take as long as you need to become comfortable with this, being deeply relaxed. It is important to feel fully relaxed as this places you in the optimum state for receiving energy and being aware of how the meditation is affecting you.

Be aware then of a deep feeling of security and attachment to your life and yourself. Be fully aware of who you are and how you are. Immerse yourself in the image and feeling of being a seed, planted in the Earth. As you continue with this you will begin to sense a feeling deep within your being. There is an irresistible urge to grow, to spread out, investigate, grow and move upwards. In your imagination and in your mind's eye.

Look upwards. From somewhere in the distance above you, you will just be able to see a light, hazy and blurred, but it beckons you towards it. You find with an effort of will, from the very core of yourself, that you can move up just a fraction towards it. As you do this, feel the goodness flowing into your body, through your feet into your veins and blood, through your skin and into your muscles, permeating every part of you. Feel this strength, energy and life flooding throughout your being.

As you continue, you will begin to note as you look up that you can sense a feeling of warmth from this light. Also, you seem to have become taller, below as well as above and you realise that your feet, like roots, have become firmly embedded into the Earth, strong now and entwined in the soil. Continue to push upwards with your will, towards the light, which grows brighter and brighter with each moment and more and more clear.

Soon it becomes lighter around you and you enter a new world. A new growth emerges from within you and you are above the surface of the Earth. Now you begin to breathe in the air above Earth. This is light, pure and clean; you taste its soft sweetness as you gladly and gratefully drink it in to your body. You feel it flowing through you, flooding your body, cleansing and purifying as it goes. Feel yourself drawn ever upwards by the Sun ad feel glad of its warmth. Allow yourself to absorb its heat and life. Soak up the Sun's rays and let yourself unfold and uncurl. Lay yourself out under the Sun and be aware of how this feels. Know that all you need is given to you for your well-being, growth and health, unconditionally.

Now the light of the Sun fades away and you begin to sense moisture in the air. It begins to rain lightly and you can open yourself still further, letting the cooling, sweet droplets of rain refresh and heal you. It is cooling and welcome. Allow yourself to drink deeply of this healing energy. Now the rain gradually stops and you are left in radiant health, flowing and radiating your energy out, in turn to all living things.

This can leave you feeling a little light headed so it is important not to use up the energy you have just generated with incoherent wanderings in your mind. Stay as long as is comfortable for you and then re-ground yourself, in the usual manner. Let the image of the plant that you are now, fade away, retaining its feeling of new-born health and life.

The technique for the Seed Meditation is as follows:

Ground and connect
Visualise yourself as seed and establish self in the Earth
Push and grow upwards until you emerge into air
Absorb rainfall and feel benefit from this
Ground

Tree Meditation

We continue our healing meditations now with a set of similar principles that we utilise, except this time placed in the image and visualisation of a tree and all its attendant benefits. As has been highlighted recently by hurricane and fights for hundreds of ancient and beautiful specimens, trees play an enormous part in our health and well-being. This is not just in their visual beauty, but in the role they play in heating, cooling and purifying air and more besides. These qualities we can absorb to ourselves in this meditation, gaining a deep identification with the tree as we do so. As such it can be an excellent idea to picture a healthy tree that you know of and like in reality and to use this in your meditation. This idea can be extended to its natural and positive conclusion by determining to care for your tree, by cleaning its immediate area, ensuring it is undamaged, feeding if necessary and so on.

Again we combine the art of visualisation with the use of healing energy. This meditation can also be used to aid ones experience, knowledge and awareness of the energies and feel the Nature of the spirits that inhabit such places, should this appeal to you as well. It can of course, be performed leaning against the tree in question, having mentally stood quietly and asked permission first.

Begin by visualising that you are standing on a path leading to a group of trees in a wood. Take time to establish the clarity of this image. Although the individual details do not matter in themselves, it is important to see and feel that you are fully there, in the wood. Walk amongst the trees becoming used to the atmosphere of the place and the energy here. Look at the different types of tree you may have in the group of trees that you have walked towards. Pause to examine some if you wish, reaching out to touch their bark if you feel so inclined.

Now pick one tree, from the image of the group you have in mind. This can be for any reason, however insignificant this may seem and whether you understand it or not. Just allow your deeper or higher mind to guide you and follow what you feel and sense is right. You should, by now, be able to do this adequately in meditation, if not your everyday life too. When you are ready, go to your tree and inwardly ask permission to work with it for this time. Do this by speaking in your mind the same as you would to anyone you respect. Do not be false. If you sense you have received confirmation to do so move closer and hug your tree, leaning in against it and letting it take your weight. Become comfortable and feel the tree trunk against your skin.

As you lean here, relax more deeply and become aware of the energy and life force in the tree. Feel this as a strong force flowing up through the tree, like its sap. Be aware of how this feels to you, leaning close against the tree. As this happens you sense now that it grows darker about you and you realise that you have merged with the tree in some way and are now inside its trunk. You are perfectly at ease here and quite safe, able to breathe easily and fully.

You become aware that you can see the tree from the inside and imagine and feel the texture from here. The trunk is the trees protection and its soul, its essence, is there with you. You in turn are part of that essence. Move your awareness down the tree and down your legs. Realise that they are one and the same. Your legs go down into the roots of the tree and into the ground. Let your awareness and the tips of your toes go down to the ends of the roots, and observe and absorb the energy there and how you feel now. Feel the strength, warmth, vitality, security and life here. Try to let yourself feel any sensation and explore.

When you are ready, begin to move up through tour tree and your body, being one and the same. Travel through the trunk of the tree and let your arms stretch upwards, into the bigger branches and then your fingers up into the smaller branches and the twigs near the top of the tree. Move slowly and gradually, following the movement with your inner awareness and noting the responses in how this feels. Keep moving up and out until you sense that you are at the very ends of the tree, the tips of your fingers at the tips of the tree. Observe how this feels and what it may be telling you.

When you are ready, imagine and feel yourself coming back to your usual height and dimensions, once more to your body, still inside the tree. Adjust to this awareness and then feel yourself slipping out of the body of the tree, as you focus on this in your mind. Focus on making a return and feel your energies separate as you become aware of yourself leaning against the tree once more. Take your time and adjust fully as you come back as this meditation can take you to quite a deep level, if you are in deep need.

Move away from the tree and pause for a moment to give your thanks. Do this silently and simply, being sincere. You may feel a little strange talking to the tree, but it isn't to the tree, so don't worry about this! When you are ready, return back through your wood the way you came until you have reached the point where you began. Now just let the place fade away and make a return to your body and your place of meditation in the usual way for you now.

The technique for the Tree Meditation is as follows:

Ground and connect
Visualise a wood and walk to a group of trees
Choose one tree that appeals to you
Move to the tree, hug it and blend with it
Move down inside the tree and then up
Absorb energy and healing
Return the way you came, from tree to you, to wood and back
Ground

Beach Meditation

This meditation utilises some basic principles that we will meet and deal with fully in the next chapter, that of the Elements, or at least some of them. The technique is very simple once again, as arguably the best meditations and things in life are. It is a simple and pleasant visualisation that can again be based on a place in reality you have visited or are lucky enough to live by. There is a basis in chemistry in this meditation that is well known. Adding (sea) salt to water is beneficial and cleansing and can be done to your regular bath. This practice is well known for purifying and cleansing the etheric layer of the aura. This meditation is indeed, an excellent one to perform in a warm bath. It can be used for treating any malady, but is especially good where there is some kind of infection.

Begin with your grounding and connecting as is usual and then visualise yourself, lying on a beach. This should be a sandy beach, but could be anywhere in the world. It is warm and sunny and you are naked. Just spend some time visualising and feeling yourself lying on the sand, your eyes closed, feeling warmed gently by the sun. The only sound you can hear is the gentle breaking of the waves that seem to come quite close to you. The sand is damp and as you lie there you feel yourself sinking into it a little. You are able to relax completely, let go of all your cares, worries and responsibilities and let the sand support your body where it lies.

There is no one else here and so you need have no fear or self-consciousness. Just take time to rest, relax and let the sun warm you. As you lie there you can hear the sound of the waves breaking closer and closer to you and soon you feel them creeping up to your feet. Continue to lie there and let the waves creep up and over your body.

The water is warm, and as it washes over you, you can feel it purifying and healing you, the salt in it cleansing your energy as well as your body. Your body feels lighter after the water has washed it, for it is free now of any dis-ease you may have been carrying with you. Simply lie there and enjoy the meditation and your healing. Let the waves continue to break gently, flowing up over your head.

You are not immersed completely, for the water is not deep enough. Instead it just gently warms, washes and heals you.

This meditation allows for much individual interpretation, so stay there for as long as you feel is necessary or until you have had enough. When this is so, the water will fade away from you and you can remain lying on the beach, letting the sun warm and dry your body. Soak up this warmth and energy for a time and when you feel ready to return, let the beach and the place fade away. Instead come back to your body and ground yourself, to return with the benefit you have gained and healing you have received.

The technique for this meditation is as follows:

Ground and Connect
Visualise beach and waves
Let waves purify and heal you
Dry yourself in the sun
Let beach fade
Ground

Purification Breath

This meditation is an excellent one to use for a wide variety of health related conditions and dis-eases. It is primarily of use for any breath and lung related disorders, giving you a chance to clear away any infection or limiting influence in these areas. The meditation can leave you a little lightheaded in the short term, so it is of course vital to perform an effective and devout grounding and connecting first, finishing with a good, clear grounding after.

The technique will leave you with a pleasant feeling of relaxation and resurgence of vital energy flow. I have known students who are smokers to have induced a bout of coughing from this technique as the energy that flows with the meditation does its work and clears out what is blocking the lungs from working properly. Whilst being in the short term unpleasant, this does have the required effect.

There is an element with this meditation of personal guidance. Each individual's breathing rate and level differs for many reasons, from diet to exercise to sleep patterns. The best guidance is therefore your own. During the meditation, you are aiming at a regular, reasonably deep pattern of breathing, with no strain or stress involved. Perhaps the simplest way to find a medium approach here is to use the Fourfold Breath pattern (see Chapter 2, if you have forgotten) for a short while before beginning the Purification Breath Itself.

You can be sitting or lying for this exercise, ensuring, as with all meditations, that you are comfortable, warm and free from distraction. To begin, perform your grounding and connecting and from the centre of balance, turn your attention to your breath. This is necessary to gain control and awareness of its function and its effect upon you. It can be most beneficial to breathe in through the nose and out through the mouth, but this will depend on your level of comfort and ease with this. Breathe easily and regularly to a comfortable level for you. Spend a little time experimenting if necessary and when you reach a satisfactory pattern, relax and let the rhythm of this take you to a deeper level of awareness. Be aware only of your breathing and its rhythm.

Now as you breathe, begin to imagine or visualise the air entering your body as you breathe in. See this as a pure, white, glowing light and energy. This should be the most pure white light that you have ever seen, perfect, crystal and full of healing power. As you breathe this in, so you absorb all the above qualities into your lungs. From here your lungs do their usual job of passing it around the body. Thus you purify your whole system and body. It can be helpful to allow your imagination to conjure up images of purity and health. Keep breathing this white light, colour and energy in and sense this pure, clean and healing air entering your body and flowing all around it, touching every part, purifying it as it goes.

If you have any specific ailment or area that you feel needs attention, it can be helpful to focus the direction of the white light to it, but you will find that there is a natural tendency for this to happen regardless. As you relax deeply, vital for the absorption of the energy, so your deeper mind will assume control and direct your conscious thought to where you need the healing most. Relax then and follow the natural direction you seem to take, trusting this process even if it is unexpected.

After a time of this (how long is entirely dependent on you – continue for as long as you want) begin to be aware also of your out breath. Imagine that you are breathing out all the negativity, disease, and pollution and rubbish from your body and specifically, your lungs. Picture this as dark, dirty and stained breath, leaving your body and flowing out and away from you. In its place comes this pure white force. You can if you wish, focus mentally on what you wish to rid yourself of, feeling this leaving you as you breathe out the dark breath.

Continue with this for as long as seems necessary for the dark breath to be gone from you and then see it gradually lightening and changing colour. Slowly it becomes first grey and then white, soon taking on the brilliance of the white light you have been breathing in. Remain breathing the white, pure force in and out, seeing yourself surrounded and filled by it. Let this be absorbed into you from all around and allow yourself to be purified. This can be a wonderful feeling, so remain with this for a little time, but not overlong. When you are ready, make your return, ensuring that you do so, refreshed and renewed, fully.

I have found that it is good to then take a drink of purified, spring water. As you slowly drink the water, see this too as a purifying and cleansing liquid, the physical counterpart of what you have just inhaled, in energy form. You could make this a daily practice to improve and generate well-being and health. Know consciously that your water is a pure source, a gift from the gods. Perhaps give your thanks for this and ask for it to be blessed, in whatever way you wish.

The technique for the Purification Breath is as follows:

Ground and connect
Establish breathing pattern
Breathe in pure white light and energy
Breathe out dark, dirty breath
Lighten dirty breath to pure white light
Ground

Pore Breathing

This exercise can be viewed as not being a meditation, but is arguably most effective when done in a meditative way, as we shall do here. It is a pleasure to do and very energising, and can make use of one's environment to great effect. If indoors, it is good to do when standing beside an open window, whatever the weather, preferably naked. Its' ideal location is perhaps on top of a hill, though here you may prefer to be clothed! It is again a very simple technique in essence that can be performed sitting, standing or lying down.

Pore Breathing produces a cleansing energy for the body and is excellent if you have any skin problems or conditions that irritate you. It can be of use when you are feeling claustrophobic, your privacy invaded, or just dirty in any way.

The meditation will leave you lighter of body and mind, which in turn will lighten your spirit.

Begin the technique by focussing on your breath and establishing a regular, natural pattern that should by now be familiar and easy to slip into. Relax deeply and do not try to manufacture a rhythm, simply let go and let it happen. Take your time here as this pattern is essential to the successful outworking of this meditation.

When you feel you are comfortable breathing in this manner, begin to imagine that as you breathe, you are breathing through every pore of your skin. There are millions of such pores, or tiny holes on your skin, which is in fact the largest organ of your body and requires looking after as much as your heart, lungs and kidneys. You may like to imagine that each one is like a tiny nose that enables you to breathe through it automatically each time your lungs take a breath. As you do, you open yourself completely, in all areas of your body, to draw in sustenance, health and life. As you breathe out you can rid yourself of that which you no longer need or want and clear your system in this way.

Continue to breathe deeply for a few minutes or for as long as seems comfortable for you and necessary to thoroughly cleanse your system through. Let sunlight, air, warmth, health and purity move fully through your body. When you have had enough simply and gently stop, coming back to full everyday awareness in the usual way, to ensure that you receive the benefits of this exercise. This meditation can leave you feeling lighter than before, so take a little time before you stand up.

The Technique for Pore Breathing is as follows:

Ground and Connect
Establish regular, natural rhythm to your breath
Breath energy in through all pores over your skin
Ground

The Healing Journey

We come now to the use of visualisation in healing meditation. For this, we undertake a guided journey, in more detail than we have so far. Tod do this use the same principles outlined previously with the Tree meditation and the meridian meditations, in following the images, as they naturally occur in your mind, as you perform the meditation. The journey takes you to a place that allows for your complete and total healing of Body, Mind and Spirit.

Remember however, that you do not need to be ill to perform this meditation. It is beneficial to do regardless of your state of health, for once in the healing place, you will always gain, even if it is just in the form of an input of energy. If you have anything wrong at all, this meditation will help. It is therefore perhaps especially helpful if you do not know the cause of your ill health or your condition is one that requires long term treatment, from a broken limb to cancer.

Visited repeatedly, the place of healing to which you go in this journey will become clearer and can come to represent a place that symbolises your perfect state of health. The more you return to it, the more you return to perfect health. If nothing else is consciously obtained, the healing journey can provide peace and comfort in the midst of a time of worry and doubt.

Begin by grounding and connecting in the usual way and becoming balanced and secure. Now begin to look out from within your imaginary (or not so imaginary!) inner, third eye. This inner vision allows you to see, as before, that which is real. As you look, you will find yourself on a path at the bottom of a hill, which slopes gently upwards before you. Around this there is thick growth of nature, but when you pause to examine it more closely, you see that it is composed of weeds, tangled and choking. There are many sharp spikes and thorns amongst them and you have to tread carefully as you begin to move along the path. Allow the image of this place to unfold naturally in your mind, accepting what you see without wonder or analysis at this stage.

The path is faint and winding, and you seem to turn this way and that as you progress. You are aware that you are climbing all the while however and have climbed further than you realise. You may spot a stream running by the side of the path in some places and when you look you see that the water is hardly flowing at all and that it is dirty and polluted.

You continue on regardless, still seeing weeds and plants that look listless and dull and still climbing the hill your path is on. To one side now, you notice a smaller path that leads off at an angle and climbs more steeply. You take this fork and follow the path, putting a little more effort into your climb now. Soon you arrive, on the precipice of a point on the hill that juts out, higher than anything else around it. Here there is a different atmosphere and the air seems somehow charged. You find a place to sit or lie down, perhaps against a tree trunk or fallen log. If you look around, there will be a place that is right for you. (If you cannot find anything, this indicates that you are not yet ready to receive your healing, so leave and return the way you came, to return when you feel ready to do so.)

Now bring to mind your dis-ease, illness, situation or whatever you require healing of or for or if nothing specific, just relax. As you focus your thoughts, you feel it begin to rain over you. The rain is warm and soon you feel wet through with it. When you look around you however, you see that this is no ordinary rain, but a rain that is filled with shimmering, rainbow-coloured droplets of liquid. It feels pleasant and refreshing and you can feel it seeping into you, all over. Stay where you are and let this healing rain wash over and through you and heal you.

Presently, when the rain stops (letting it do this of its own accord) stand up once more and begin to make your return. Tread slowly and carefully back down the steep path to where the fork is. Then return back down the side of the hill. Now the going seems much easier and the path straighter. Pause here and there to look. When you do, you will see that the weeds have gone and in their place there is vibrant growth, full of flowers and dazzling colours. You seem to notice a deeper resonance from the colours than you have ever seen before and even the grass looks flowing and healthy. The stream is clear now and flowing freely. It seems as if everything is in a state of radiance and bliss. There is a lightness to your being and your step as you return and soon you are back where you began.

Let the image of this place fade away and know that you can return when you wish. If you are treating a long term condition, you may find that little by little the weeds become less and less as you climb the path as the place mirrors your return to health. Return then in the usual way, grounding clearly and fully before opening your eyes.

The technique for the Healing Journey is as follows:

Ground and connect
Visualise path and weeds around you
Climb to fork in path and then to precipice
Let rainbow rain fall over and through you
Return, seeing new growth and healing around you
Ground

Sleep Meditation

It may seem strange to be including a meditation with the title of Sleep, but experience has shown me that this is an area that causes a great deal of trouble in maintaining our health and well-being. Our sleep time needs to be a quality one for in it we rest, recover and regenerate ourselves at the most basic energy level. To deprive ourselves of this natural state is to deprive ourselves of health at its most basic level.

There can be many reasons for the deprivation of sleep, whether artificially induced or not. This is mentioned for the slumber induced by drugs or alcohol is not a natural, regenerating kind of sleep but a state in which the body is artificially put to rest for a time. The same goes for the use of sleeping tablets, all too widespread and easy it seems. What is required is a means by which we can cease the endless chatter of thoughts in our minds while we stare into the darkness wishing we could sleep. We need a means by which we can gently and naturally drift into a restful state of sleep, to wake refreshed and rested and ready to deal with the day as best we can.

This meditation concerns itself with that goal. It is a meditation technique that is easy and simple, occupying the mind on one simple focus and thereby enabling it to remain relaxed, but not full of meaningless chatter. From this relaxed state of mind we relax the body and so slip into sleep. It may be worthwhile mentioning here that we often subconsciously deprive ourselves of sleep for a good reason. It is during sleep that the deeper levels of our mind are free to communicate to us, in a language that always gives us truth. If we are not yet ready to deal with the truth we may not wish to sleep and so face reality, in this way. Consequently, our conscious mind invents things – usually problems and worries – that prevent us from sleeping. It is at the above deeper levels that a change in consciousness occurs that allows for us to awake, knowing an answer, feeling different about our problems, for subconsciously, we now know the answer required. With this comes responsibility, never easy to accept.

The sleep meditation lets you reach that state whereby changes in consciousness can occur naturally and easily. It is of course, best performed lying in bed, or wherever one wishes to sleep! Grounding and Connecting is not necessary for the objective here is very different. Simply let your eyes close and take a deep breath or two to relax yourself init6ially. Then gently focus on your breathing, letting go of all control over this so as to allow a natural state to take over. Just let go and let this happen by itself. If this is a problem at any time, use the fourfold breath to gain control first, then let go from there.

Now focus your concentration in a relaxed way, on your feet. Let them go limp and imagine that the outline becomes less defined as you relax deeply. Feel them become weightless. Visualise your feet spreading out so that it becomes unclear where your body ends and the energy around you begins. Your feet are now relaxed fully and weightless, drifting just a little above the bed. From here work up through your body in the same manner.

Move your focus up to your knees, relaxing your lower legs in the same manner and imagining them becoming weightless as before. Now repeat the procedure for the upper legs, pelvis, waist, torso, hands, arms, shoulders, neck and face. By now you are free and light, floating in the air above your bed. From here just let your mind drift to an awareness of how light your body is, how it has merged with the energy all around you. Then just let go and drift into sleep, if you are not there already by now. It is quite common once you are familiar with the method of this meditation, to get no more than halfway before you succumb to sleep.

This meditation facilitates the necessary brain wave pattern that enables sleep. When we sleep for, say, six hours, this consists of four 90 minute cycles of alpha, theta and delta wave patterns, as they are called. These are your brain waves, the energy from your brain, moving at different speeds that relate to and control different functions in your body's system.

Beta, your conscious, 'everyday' pattern is not used during sleep as it relates to the five senses used during waking. Alpha, theta and delta relate to the spiritual and higher realms. These patterns are regulated by the right, intuitive hemisphere of the brain whilst beta waves relate to the left, conscious and logical side.

The technique for the Sleep Meditation is as follows:

Relax and let of breathing
Focus on your feet and allow to become weightless
Work up through your head in the same way
Sleep!!

This brings us to the end of the Healing meditations. From here on we turn our attention to the use of meditation as an aid to development through life, perhaps assuming that you are by now a regular meditator and have consciously realised and utilised its benefits in your life. Now then, the real work begins!

Chapter 7 – Personal Development

Having acquired the habit and technique of meditation in one's life, it is now possible to take things a stage further and explore the subject in more depth and put it to a greater use. This involves specific meditations geared towards developing Body, Mind and Spirit. There are many approaches to this, meditation often providing a core or backbone of a greater work. Here we look at the use of meditation as the skin as well as the core of our development, for meditation can apply to the deeper, inner levels as much as it can to the more surface, tangible ones.

To utilise the practice of meditation in personal development it is really necessary to practice daily. This allows for a regular established time for reflection, for objective awareness, which allows for the change in consciousness that in turn allows for the decisions to be made that are the external indicator of some level of development. It has been said that change is the only evidence of life and so our lives must reflect the inner changes meditation brings about on that level. Our lives and society today are such that at least one daily period in meditation is necessary if we are to truly remain in control and in charge of all that influences ourselves and our lives. There is such a barrage of information, speed and activity required to us to be a functioning part of society that we must, at some point, step aside from the whirl of all this, to ask ourselves; what is going on, why am I doing this and for what purpose?

These questions can perhaps form all that is necessary for effective personal development meditation, asked with an honest objectivity, but it is at this point that we meet with a 'Catch 22' style problem. Such is the amount of thoughts, feelings, actions and myriad other things cascading around in our minds, from our work, families, homes, cars, books we read, films we see, music we hear and to a surprisingly large degree, advertisements broadcast at us, that it becomes very difficult for the modern mind to disregard this on cue, each day. Thus we are unable to step aside from the very objectives that we are vainly trying to develop through our lives, because of the pressure on us to do just that. We must first of course distinguish between genuine development and simply following the dictates and emotions induced by advertising and so on, but that is a duty to which I cannot aspire to teach you via the medium of this book (tempting as it is to try!).

It therefore becomes necessary to provide a focus for the mind to stop it drifting into endless repetition of thoughts along the lines of 'I must remember to set the video' or 'I'll cook dinner as soon as I've finished this', whilst you are doing your meditation. This is all too often the case when we try to simply spend time meditating and nothing more. Unless you have become very proficient and have been following every urge to meditate more through this book, it is, with all honesty, unlikely that you will be able to just sit and meditate, emptying your mind of all its daily rubbish long enough to produce anything of value, in terms of personal development.

Since this book is intended to be a practical approach to the daily use of meditation in modern Western society, we must therefore provide a framework for our meditations that enables us to set aside the daily whirl and instead focus on these forces and energies – that which underlies and shapes the reality we experience – and so regain the greater control and awareness necessary to provide the sought after change of consciousness. In other worlds, we need a way to check what, how, why and where, we are going in our lives and thereby give ourselves the chance to change it if we deem it necessary.

This follows a principle that again echoes why a daily practical meditation approach is so vital to a full and progressive life. It is so very easy to accept the easy option of rolling up to work, getting through the day, getting dinner out of the way and spending the evening before the television, perhaps with one evening out a week. There is a great deal of unspoken, subtle pressure to live this way, as 'respected members of society' that it takes a degree of motivation and will all too unusual to break and remain free of the deadly traps of respectability and 'doing the right thing'. You need only do the right thing by yourself and meditation can, surprisingly, enable you to discover what that is and how to do it. Often, it is the very thing that you have always dreamed about but never thought you were capable of. Meditation provides the framework around which you can construct your own life, with your own challenges, lessons, failures, triumphs and ultimately learning and fulfilment.

It is therefore logical to turn to the very framework on which our lives are built and based, to enable and assure ourselves that we are the ones in control of all we think, say, feel and do. Humanity has for thousands of years looked to the Elements for the explanation of life and to see and understand its methods. More recently, we have tried, foolishly and vainly, to master and control these Elements. This is a pointless quest which humanity, through the 20th century, has stubbornly refused to drop. Instead, in the name of progress, we have as a race, killed much of what we have been trying to control, to the level that we now threaten our own survival. This is not only that we threaten the Earth, but that the Earth effectively threatens us. Not out of spite or anger, but simply out of her own survival instincts.

We are increasingly shown the power and magnitude of these Elements, recalling such events as the Sydney fires, the Mississippi floods, numerous earthquakes and the English hurricane of 1987. Such have been the awesome manifestations of the powers of Fire, Water, Earth and Air respectively that we must surely learn the lessons the above shows us, or perish. One such way is to accept that the Elements are bigger and stronger than we are and in the accepting, learn to co-operate and utilise these forces for our survival and development, not at the expense of technology, but by adapting it. But what has all this to do with practical meditation?

In fact it has everything to do with practical meditation. If you now re-read the above paragraph in the context of the Elements being those forces that not only shape and control life on Earth as a planet and for humanity as a race, then you can begin to see how vital and necessary it becomes to see their workings in your own self and life. Thus we discover that we need to see how these Elements are affecting us at any one time and so establish a marriage with them, thereby giving each of us the control we seek. The greater the awareness of the Elements at the inner level of meditation provides for us the ability to see their effect and working, of their respective spheres of influence. From this we can construct and re-construct as necessary, at the most basic level, ourselves and our lives, as we absorb the experiences so mercilessly thrown at us. In reign over us, confident and sure in the knowledge that by separating ourselves from their influence for a time, each day in meditation, we can observe what is happening to us, how it is happening and why, and so take steps to learn from this. Meditation is therefore, eminently practical.

It is now necessary to see and understand how each of the Elements affect us and constitute a part of us, so that we are in a position to do something about them. Much has been written on the nature of and correspondences to the Elements, all of which add to the understanding. What is given here is again the briefest of introductions, sufficient for our purposes, but for those readers who require further stimulus, I recommend Marian Green's work 'The gentle Arts of Aquarian Magic', which gives four excellent chapters on the nature of the Elements.

The four Elements are Earth, Air, Fire and Water. For those already wondering, the fifth Element, that of Spirit, is dealt with after these four elements have been examined and meditated upon. Perhaps the simplest and most directly applicable way of describing their nature is by the four classifications of practical, mental, spiritual and emotional, respectively.

It is to these four areas that we turn in our Element meditations as the means for analysing and controlling our everyday lives. We need to gain an awareness of our actions, thoughts, beliefs and feelings, above our ordinary level if we are to progress and develop them. The means by which we do that is by meditating upon them. If you will allow me the luxury of one potential 'cop-out' here, you will find that the best way to a deeper understanding of how each Element affects you, is by first studying the meditations and secondly, doing them!   This is because the content of the meditations is in some degree symbolic. That is to say that what you see and feel during the visualisation journeys are a representation of what you are experiencing in yourself and life from that particular Element.

It is again very much for you to analyse what you experience during these meditations for yourself. My only advice and guidance here is to be honest and truthful. I have not listed the technique for these meditations, as this is simply to ground and connect, follow the journey and ground again.

Earth Journey

Begin, as you should by now expect, with your Grounding and Connecting. It is at this level of meditation that this becomes truly the introductory procedure that is however, still vital for your safe and successfully journeying.

From the centre of balance, imagine that you are looking out from within that same, inner and Third eye that you have previously used. You can spend a little time focussing on this, from within your forehead. This will open the energy centre or chakra there and you may feel any of the 'energy sensations' of tingling, heat etc. Imagine that this eye opens and looks out, seeing what is true and real, but at another level of perception.

As you look, focus on a path in a wood. The wood is thick with trees and ahead of you there is a setting sun. You can hear the sound of woodland life coming alive for the evening and night around you. Birds call in the trees and close by you can hear the sound of animals scurrying about in search of food.

If you look closer amongst the vines and bushes you may catch a glimpse of movement in the dry leaves and grasses that carpet the floor of this place. There is a dry heat present, at the end of a hot day and as you begin to walk along the path, the sound of your movement alarms some of the birds who take flight with a flurry of beating wings.

As you walk you can begin to sense the very thick and almost solid atmosphere in this place. Everything around you seems somehow to be more real. Follow the path along, no more than a rough track that has been worn into the ground, perhaps by other pairs of feet who have trodden this way in years before you.

The path turns this way and that through the woods and as you walk your eyes become more and more accustomed to the fading light. You find that you are able to pick out great detail around you. The path straightens out now and the trees, previously of many types but now tall and straight form what seems to be an impenetrable wall either side of you. Looking up, you can just see far above you that the branches form an arch and you feel the air changing as you continue to follow this avenue. You find now that you have a feeling deep within your being and self that comforts you, something you know you have felt before, but cannot quite recall.

It seems to you that you are going down and looking ahead it appears that the path does slope down. Large boulders with tufts of grass between are interspersed between the trees and the path is strewn with loose stones, causing you to pick your way carefully. Soon there are no trees alongside you, only rock, sloping steeply up beside you. The path is now solid rock too. You look down at your feet to tread carefully, as you continue your walk.

After a short time, you realise that you have been travelling down for a long distance. As you look above you see that the rock has joined and you are in a tunnel, beneath the Earth. You can see quite clearly however, so long as you concentrate and focus, your eyes being used to the dark now. A little way ahead of you there is a dim light and you move towards this.

Your feet seem to become increasingly heavy as the path continues down. The light ahead of you is not bright but it comforts you with its presence. As you come closer to the light the path emerges into a cave. You realise that you are deep within the body of the Earth. Look around you now and see that all that is in the cave is a table or altar in the centre, carved beautifully out of the rock. On its surface burns a small flame, still and steady, the source of the light you followed. In the shadows around you can see symbols and pictures painted on the walls of the cave. Pause now to study your surroundings, the pictures and symbols, and your feelings at being here. Take as long as you need at this stage and when you feel ready, continue.

Now move over to the altar and take a seat before it. There is a shaped depression in the rock that gives you a comfortable seat. Looking at the altar you can see objects, some from the woods, placed upon it. You close your eyes as the atmosphere seems to close in around you, making you feel warm, safe and comfortable. You have a feeling of sinking. For a time all is quiet and still as you seem to dream of the Earth, beneath the cave. Now just allow any feeling and images to come to you as they will, for as long as you wish or need to.

When you are ready feel yourself rising up once more and sense yourself back in the cave. Open your eyes and see the altar before you. You may notice that all seems somehow different, more alive than before. Look again at the walls as you may understand what you see more now.

It is time now for you to leave, knowing that you can return when you wish, to experience the cave and the Earth again and to learn more. Now retrace your steps coming at your own pace back up the rock path to the avenue of trees. Gradually it becomes brighter and you can see a weird glow around you as you emerge back into the woods.

Looking up, you see the moon hanging in a clear sky and from somewhere you hear the howl of a wolf, but you are comforted by this, not frightened. The moonlight guides you back through the twist and turns of the path back to where you recognise your starting point. Now let this place fade from you, bringing with you what you have learnt. Bring your attention back to your breath and ground in the usual manner.

Air Journey

Begin this journey in the same manner as before, by grounding yourself and focussing your attention on the third eye area, imagining that you see from here. When you look you will see that you are standing at the foot of a steep path, which climbs up the side of a cliff. There is a stony beach beside you, leading to a calm sea, some distance from you. Looking up you can see the white faces of the cliff, rough and weather-beaten by years of exposure. As you look a little closer, you can see the route the path takes, as it turns this way and that, weaving its way to the top of the cliff. You can feel a cool and pleasant sea breeze blowing across your face, and you can smell and taste the sea air as you breathe. You stand for a moment and just breathe in this purifying air, taking a good lung full and letting it circulate around your body, cleansing and purifying as it goes.

After a short time you turn your eyes back to the path ahead of you and begin to move forward. You find that you need to tread quite carefully as the path is steep and there are some lumps of chalk from the cliffs lying here and there. You feel yourself rising above the sea quite quickly however, yet the cliff still looms large above you.

As you continue your climb you turn first one way and then the other as the twists and turns of the path leave you feeling a little dizzy and confused. The wind picks up too, blowing your hair across your face and making it a little awkward each time you turn to face it. You lean forwards to make the going easier and dig in with your heels as you climb further up the cliff.

You pause a moment now to catch your breath and look to the cliffs' top. You strain your eyes, but cannot make out the green edge of the grass that marked the summit. It seems as if everything has become hazy about you. You realise that the clouds have come down over the cliffs and are beginning to swirl about you. Bracing yourself against the increasing force of the wind, you continue to follow the path up the side of the cliff.

As you climb you feel the coolness of the wind reaching into your body, but this is refreshing rather than unpleasant. The wind is strong enough at times however to cause you to steady yourself to maintain your balance. You instinctively reach out to the side of the cliff and its damp texture is strong and solid against your grasp. You press on, only just able to see ahead of you now, so thick is he cloud. The wind comes in gusts and swirls now that seem to catch your breath and carry it over the cliff.

Just when you think that you cannot go any further, as the wind begins to bite, you feel the path level out beneath your feet and then the softness of lush grass. Next the cloud clears a little and you can see and realise that you have reached the top of the cliff. The cloud moves back around you and you can see grass and bracken about your feet. There is a small clump of trees, leaning to one side as if they point out to sea, pushed that way by force of the wind as they have grown.

You follow the direction of the trees and look towards the sea. The wind blows very strongly at you, but from behind. As you turn to face the sea you find that you can breathe easily and feel the wind whipping through your bones. You raise your arms above you in a gesture of surrender to the wind. As you do so you feel yourself sway slightly and for a moment you wonder if it will carry you away.

Then the gust subsides and you feel the wind release you. As it does you become aware of a lightness not present before. You stay in that position for a short time now and allow the wind to blow all your cobwebs away, purifying and cleansing body, mind and spirit. Surrender to that force and feel all that you are holding on to, all that prevents clarity, lifting away and being taken out to sea.

When you are ready and in your own time, bring your arms down. You have a feeling of being much lighter, as if you are floating now. You can see nothing around you now, for you are surrounded by thick cloud. Now look down and you will see only cloud beneath you. The feeling of movement and floating comes back to you and you realise with a rush of exhilaration that you have been lifted up by the cloud and have moved out over the edge of the cliff, above the sea.

You feel perfectly safe and have no sense of alarm. Instead the cloud supports you and there is a feeling of safety and freedom, as if the cloud is hugging and comforting you. Close your eyes and submit to this feeling. You have the slow sensation of descending gradually. Allow a short time to elapse in your meditation now, enjoying the floating and drifting, seeing where you will be carried.

Soon you feel a surface beneath your feet and you see that the cloud has become wispy thin. You look down and see pebbles beneath you, on which you stand. The cloud has brought you back to the beach at the foot of the cliff and has now dispersed. Facing the cliff you can feel a gentle, warm breeze blowing in off the sea, which is pleasing to you. As you stand there is a lightness of body and a clarity of mind not present before. Aware only of this, let the cliff and the beach fade away and make your return ensuring that you ground fully.

Fire Journey

Begin with grounding and connecting and looking out once more from within that inner eye. This time you find yourself sitting before a candle in a room that has a familiarity for you. It seems as if you have been here before, but you can only recall the scene dimly. The room is curiously shaped, having several sides. Each side is coloured with a mixture of reds and oranges that blend into each other, the deepest red at the bottom to the palest orange at the top, that gives way then to white. As you look around the room it has a dazzling effect on you, leaving you a little disoriented and light-headed. You also notice the temperature in the room is very warm.

Your gaze returns to the candle and you see that it is made of the same colours as the walls of this room. The flame burns brightly and seems almost alive as you haze at it. It dances and flickers this way and that and seems to hold you spellbound. You allow yourself to be taken in by its spell and as you sit and gaze at the candle flame, you become aware of how calm you have become. All that you can see now are the movements of the flame and it seems to respond to your thoughts. You realise now that a contact has been made and that you can communicate with the living being of this flame. Formulate any questions in your mind now and let the flame show you the answers. If you prefer, simply sit, be still and allow images, thoughts, worlds and feelings to emerge from the flame.

After a short while your concentration is broken by the smell of smoke that drifts across to you. You turn your gaze around and see behind you for the first time in this room, a door. This is open now and smoke drifts in. You sniff the smoke and can smell herbs and resin within it. You then notice the crackling sound of burning and decide to see what type of fire it is.

Stand up now and go to and through the door. You come into a grassed area, with flint walls on all sides. The light is fading and the brightness of the fire glows more and more with each passing moment. You stand to take in your surroundings and look more closely. You become conscious of two small walls of flame, burning steadily upwards in front of you, for a distance of some 30 metres.

149

They are spaced about six feet apart. Lining the floor is a carpet of glowing coals, red hot.

You move over to stand before the burning coals, at the centre of the walkway. The flames reach up to your waist either side. They give off plumes of smoke that go spiralling off into the air. You watch as the smoke rises and swirls about you, lifting you up it seems, with its strong fragrance. You breathe this in and it seems to swirl about your head. As you stand at the edge of the walkway, the heat from the flames and coals and the fragrance, reach out and surround you. Your thoughts turn to the fire within you and you feel the force of this rising inside you. As you stand watching the glowing embers, the force grows and grows inside you and seems to make your muscles burn.

The force within continues and compels you to move forward. Something clicks inside your head and everything comes into focus. From nowhere you see the image of a burning candle. At a quick but light pace you move, your eyes never leaving the burning candles. You move closer, unaware of anything but the candle. You are focussed and true, each step taking you closer and closer to your goal. This is all you see and all you know. For these few moments you have a clarity of mind and purpose you have not known before. For a while time stops and realisation comes to you.

When you become aware again of where you are, you find yourself back in the fire-coloured room from where you began, sitting before the candle once more. You realise you have walked the way of fire and have trodden the burning coals. You have emerged unscathed and undamaged. Now there is peace and stillness and calm from the steadily burning candle flame before you.

As you look at the flame, you feel a perfect calm within both mind and body. The colours and light fade around you and in its place your awareness switches to your breath. From here let the room fade completely and bring yourself back, grounding fully.

Water Journey

Begin in the usual way, grounding and connecting then focussing on the inner sight of the third eye. Look from within and see yourself in the middle of a dense forest. All around you are large-leafed trees, each and every one as you look, with droplets of water glistening and shining on the polished surface of the leaves. As you look about you some more, you see all kinds of unusual, tropical plants. The flowers of some may be familiar, while others amaze you with their fantastic display of colour. It is humid here and damp. You clothes soon become wet through with the light but persistent rainfall that makes it more pleasant. There are exotic scents that drift to you as you begin to walk about and explore this place.

You begin to move through the forest, finding that you have to push your way through the leaves and branches. Some of them spring back into your face with a wet slap and soon you are wet through. The ground beneath your feet is soft and springy and damp too. You hear the sounds of the forest around you as you walk, birds calling and unseen animals rustling.

You make your way along, squeezing between trees and ducking low to avoid overhanging branches. Continuing along you begin to hear the sound of running water. It is distant at first and you can see nothing of its source, only the forest around you. Your course takes you closer to the sound however which grows louder. Still you continue but still you cannot see the water that makes the noise. This has grown to be a constant roar in your ears and as you push your way through the leaves, all at once the forest stops.

You find yourself then standing on the banks of a large and fast flowing river. This sound is loud and the sight grips and holds you. The water froths and bubbles, against the banks and against the occasional boulder that juts out of the water. As you stand and watch you see a branch being carried along in the foam of the water surface. The sight and sound of the river seems to overwhelm you as you stand there and brings feelings and emotions flooding up. You are constantly splashed as the river flows by your feet. You are not bothered by this as the force of the river seems to grip you, filling you with emotion and exhilaration.

All at once the feelings sweeps over you and without a thought of the consequences you jump in. There is a splash and for a second the water closes above you. Then there is light and air and you bob up above the surface. The force of the water carries you along and instinctively you thrash out with your arms and legs. The more you do this however, the bumpier and more unpleasant your ride seems to get. Soon you give up your struggle and let go and submit to the water and the feelings that seem to well up within you and are carried away for a time.

Soon you become aware of a new sound. With some effort you adjust your position, still being carried along by the river, to look ahead of you. A short distance ahead, the river disappears and a great wash of spray rises in its place. The forest either side seems to vanish too and you can see only sky beyond. You become conscious of a great roar that fills your heart. You brace yourself to fall over the edge of what you now realise is a waterfall. Almost as you do this, the support and closeness of the river leaves you and you feel yourself tumbling over the edge.

To your surprise, you find that it is not like falling. You are breathless, but are aware only of the water showering around you. This seems to wash you, somehow inside as well as all over your body. You let yourself be carried down by the water and as you do so, you feel a release and letting go emotionally too.

Soon there is a gentle splash and you land in a pool of water. You are carried away from the waterfall so that its sound becomes gentle and distant. Here there is calm and quiet, with the gentle lapping of this pool onto the Earth. Catching your breath and your senses, you are taken by the water and come to a gentle rest on a grass verge. You are at the foot of cliffs in a still and quiet haven.

You have given yourself to the water kingdom and now feel the calm after the storm. You climb up out of the water and lie on the grass.

The lapping of the water on the bank calms you and you close your eyes, feeling emotionally fulfilled and released. Gradually now, this place fades away from you and you become aware again of where you are. Bring your thoughts back to your breath and slowly deepen this, grounding yourself and returning in the usual, thorough manner.

Spirit Journey

The fifth Element of Spirit was mentioned earlier and I will just take a moment now to clarify its existence, for many choose to ignore or forget about it. For this clarification, we turn to the holistic principle of the whole being greater than the sum of the parts. Applied to the Elements, this means that when we combine the four Elements as we have seen them, we get the resulting quintessence of the fifth Element of Spirit or Ether. This is taken as referring to the higher spirituality inherent in each being and to their divine nature, in whatever form envisaged it may take.

It may be of note to mention here that we, as humans, are a combination of the other four Elements and need each of them, in different ways to survive. As such, in that we are that combination, we are Spirit personified. This of course means that if we try to control and master the four Elements by suppression, we are really trying to suppress the human and divine spirit. History shows us time and again, that the human spirit cannot be supressed.

The beach described that you travel to in this journey is based on one that I was fortunate to visit, in the former Yugoslavia, on the Adriatic coast, where on occasions I would watch the dolphins playing in the early morning sun sparkling magically on water that was as clear as a perfect diamond. Such images lodge themselves in the mind to be cherished and opened like the pages of a favourite photograph book. This then is one of mine which I share with you and hope that you find and treasure your own.

Begin in the usual manner and when you are ready look from the inner eye. Now you find that you are standing before a small gate, between a wooden fence that runs alongside a field. The field is behind you and ahead of you. Beyond that gate and sloping down from where you stand is a beautiful beach. You can smell the fresh, sea air from where you stand and feel the breeze blowing in from the sea. The day is warm, but with patches of cloud over an otherwise blue sky. The ground beneath your feet is warm and damp, as if there has been recent rainfall. Becoming accustomed to this place, you feel a certain inner response deep in your heart that compels you forward.

Reach down now and open the gate, stepping down the stony and sloping path that you find on the other side. Above you, you can hear the call of seagulls and pause to follow the swooping paths they take in the air currents. There is sand scattered on the path now, amongst the weathered rock and clumps of grass jutting out here and there. As you make your way down the slope, the path makes its way through a cleft in the rock that is taller than you. Ahead you can see the beach, where the small cliff ends. Here there is no wind and all seems quiet for a few moments, save for the distant breaking of the waves on the shore.

Soon you come to the end of the path between the rocks and your feet on to the deep sand, interspersed here and there with pebbles. Remove your shoes now, leaving them at the end of the path where you know they will be safe. Stepping out of them, you put your feet down on the sand, feeling them sink and the fine grains coming up through your toes. Make your way forward now, towards the water, treading carefully between the stones and pebbles. The sound of the sea comes to you now and grows clearer as your feet move into the deep sand where waves have recently reached. Now the salty air blows over your face and body and you can taste it too as you breathe deeply of its cleansing and refreshing quality.

As you stand there, almost without noticing you have walked into the edge of the sea and the waves are gently breaking about your feet and ankles. The water is pleasantly warm and you let your eyes close. You are quite alone and there is no fear. Take a deep breath now of that fresh sea air and let the breeze blow over your body. Feel the waves breaking against your legs and feel the warm, wet sand as you sink into it a little where you stand.

As you stand on the beach with your eyes closed, the Sun then comes out from behind a cloud and suddenly you feel the warmth of its rays penetrating your body. It seems to hold you and time too seems to stop. All that exists is the damp sand, the sea, the salty air and the Sun. All at once you let go from within, letting go of all your thoughts and all your feelings, leaving all tension in your body behind. As you do so, you feel a deep peace come over you and you are held, spellbound and floating, in a timeless place of exhilaration and wonder.

Let yourself experience this peace now and as you do so, find the understanding that comes with it. Feel the presence and power within that you know also is outside, in the sand, the water, the air and the Sun. Feel your intrinsic connection with all things, realise that you are a part of all things and know that they are part of you, as you are part of them. Pause now and let yourself feel and be aware.

After a time you feel the Sun's warmth leave your body and opening your eyes you see that it has gone behind another cloud. The air seems to have turned a little colder now and the breeze is a little stiffer. You realise too, on looking down, that the tide has gone out and the sea no longer reaches your feet. Lifting your legs you shake yourself free of the damp sand and turn away from the beach.

As you move, you feel a lightness in your body and a feeling and awareness in your being that was not present before. This sensation is comforting to you and you know that something inside you has changed and that you will never be quite the same again.

Make your way back up the beach now, back on the dry sand, beginning to pick your way carefully between the pebbles and stones once more. The sound of the breaking waves fades away and you see the path ahead of you, between the cleft in the rock. When you reach the beginning of the path, you see that your shoes are just as you left them. Put these on now and continue your journey through the rock. The path slopes upward now and soon you can see the fence and the gate, with the field behind it.

The gate has not been touched since you left it and when you reach it now, open it and step through. Closing the gate behind you, you are back in the field where you began. Now allow this place to fade away, knowing that you can return whenever you wish. Return then, bringing with you the inner transformation and feeling of power within. Come back slowly, grounding in the usual way, and having let the field fade from you.

It will have been seen that these meditations all include an aspect that we have not met before in our travels through the subject. At certain times in each of the above meditations it can be seen that the power of the Element takes control and there is a pause in the text. Here you are required only to let your mind wander where it will, having previously focussed it loosely on whichever Element is being considered. A relaxed awareness is all that is required for this and a little trust and confidence in what you are doing! Given this, it is surprising what the mind can come up with, when simply meditating on the subject of nature of water and the feelings you associate with it, for example. This technique can be repeated as often as you wish also, for what you consider in your meditation is dependent on how you are at the time it is performed. This of course, changes each time.

It is perhaps worth mentioning here that it is this same technique of loose focus, than can be utilised to meditate on a piece of text, prose or poetry. The mind, having been relaxed previously is left to wander at will over the subject, revealing all manner of different aspects of meaning inherent in the text being studied. The type of text chosen will depend greatly on each individual, but many choose the great spiritual texts of the world, such as 'Tao Te Ching' or more latterly Kahlil Gibran's *'The Prophet'* or similar. This is of course our choice, but does lead us nicely on to our next Chapter.

Chapter 8 – Spiritual Development

Astute readers may recall my saying at the beginning of this book that it is one of practical, down-to-earth meditation, with little to do with the 'instant enlightenment' methods available, or for that matter, those that take longer to get you floating! Why then, are you now reading a chapter entitled 'Spiritual Development'?

My justification for this is simple. It is my experience from my years meditating and teaching its practice, that those that are drawn to do so often have an underlying interest in or awareness of, some kind of spiritual belief, awareness or method. I must stress at this stage that how you choose to demonstrate or apply the particular spiritual beliefs you may have is entirely your own choice (or should be!) and that the meditations given in this book will not interfere with them or dictate, in any way. Since experience has shown me that those who graduate to a regular meditation practice in their lives are prone to an increased spiritual awareness, it is only fair, if other readers will forgive me, to offer them something by which they can further this new found part of themselves.

Of course it may be nothing more than a psychological curiosity that prompts the seeker to turn to spiritual subjects, brought about by the known association meditation has with this field. This cannot be argued against and all I will say in this context is that if this is the case, in my experience this indicates a deep need, whether acute or not, within that individual, that meditation might just go some way to meeting. The salient point here is that meditation may not give that individual all their answers, but it can and will, if allowed time, show the person the correct path to the correct answer for them.

Included in this short Chapter are two meditations, *The Sanctuary* and *Meeting Your Guides*. I have found that *The Sanctuary* meditation which follows, though it is here classed as spiritual development, is extremely effective and valuable as a therapeutic regular meditation to perform. It has much in common with practices used in hypnosis (the main difference between these two subjects being that in meditation you are still in control) and as such comes with my strongest recommendation to learn and use it, for I feel that it can become one of the most valuable meditation techniques you can perform. *Meeting Your Guide* then utilises the Sanctuary you have created to meet your own guide.

Meditation is used in a great many religious or spiritual practices and in a great many different ways. Its definition differs greatly across the world and its use varies equally in books written on the subject. Here we stick to the same use of meditation that we have utilised throughout the book – that of a practical approach that integrates rather than separates the spiritual from the material.

The Sanctuary

The Sanctuary meditation is basically a guided journey to a place that will serve you, for a lifetime if necessary, as your own unique place. This is yours to visit whenever you wish, for whatever purpose you wish. It may be used for escape, simply as a place of rest and relaxation, for personal contemplation and reflection and just as a simple and familiar way of getting away from the world for a time.

This practise of 'meditational escapism' is fine so long as you do not allow it to become an escape from reality and seek instead to replace the material reality and life you have with an imaginary one.

The Sanctuary can also be a place to visit as a gateway to a deeper or higher level of meditation. This is done by following the guided journey to your Sanctuary and from there following a technique such as the Pink Bubble for example, which will then be performed at a deeper level than your Sanctuary allows. It is for this reason and in this method that we use the Sanctuary for the higher purpose of spiritual development in the meditation for meeting your guide.

The Sanctuary is a place that in time becomes alive within your psyche. As such it provides a solid and real inner place where you can view yourself and your life objectively. Since in the meditation you re instructed to create and visualise what would be the most perfect place for you imaginable, it follows that here you need have no other concern, save that which you choose to focus on. The Sanctuary is therefore just that, a safe refuge from your troubles, cares and woes. Here you can detach yourself from them and decide what it is that you really want or need to do.

The meditation, when it is spoken aloud by a teacher, takes you as far as the door of your Sanctuary. Once inside you are on your own, for it is your place and no suggestion as to its contents should be given. The essence of the Sanctuary is partly in its uniqueness and individuality and so this should not be interfered with in any way. There are however a few pointers given here as ideas on which you may like to work or develop. It is vital however that you choose what you want to be in your Sanctuary, and no other.

The Sanctuary can basically exist anywhere and any how you want it to. At the deep or high level at which we are now operating in meditation, logic does not apply. Consequently, if you wish to have trees with purple bark or bricks with yellow spots, you can! All that is necessary is that you stick to what is the most perfect place for you, as it is this identification that you need to make in your mind with your Sanctuary, if it is to become that.

The Sanctuary may be one room, several rooms, a whole house or even a tent. It could be inside or outside, a bit of each, or have a way of getting from one to the other. It may be based on a place you know or have visited, or indeed wish to visit. It may have one aspect of such a place, but the rest is imaginary.

The sanctuary is like you mind and has many levels and images that may come to you. It is in this sense, a reflection of your own mental self and state and in saying this it is vital that you realise that it is you and only you that controls this. As such, it is you and you only that can create and destroy your Sanctuary and any part of it.

Once you have created your Sanctuary in your mind, you are at complete liberty to change it. This can be completely or only one tiny detail or anything in between. It is advisable not to continue changing the whole thing too often or it will lack stability and you will not be able to get used to its energy and atmosphere and so reach the deeper and higher levels possible. If you feel you need to change your Sanctuary completely, it is best to do this early on in its development and allow the correct one to form in your mind. Of course your Sanctuary may be a place that is subject to change naturally, if it is outside and you like the change of the seasons. Of course it can still be outside but stay in leaf, falling leaves, buds or whatever, all year round, year in, year out. It is truly a place beyond time and not subject to the laws of nature unless you want it to be.

Another aspect in creating your Sanctuary is not to try to make too many choices, based on what your heart or your head is telling you. Try instead to just allow it to form itself as the deeper levels of what your being knows better than your logical mind or unstable heart what you like most and more importantly, what you need most. Trust your intuition and mind then to present a place or part of a place to you and then build on this. One way that you can do this is to follow the meditation without prior consideration or thought, enter through the door and just see what is there and adapt accordingly. This may take a little confidence or trust in your meditational abilities but is perhaps the purest and truest way to reach a Sanctuary.

This is also true of the contents of your Sanctuary, which again can be no more or less than you want them to be. The smallest details can make a difference to the feeling of your Sanctuary and so it is important to have only what you wish to have there. It should not however become a place that is filled with all the material goods that you long for but know that you cannot have. Leave such wish fulfilment for the movies to do that for you!

161

It can be a sensible idea not to divulge the contents of your Sanctuary in detail to many people. A discussion or comparison with a close and trusted friend is perfectly acceptable, but it is not a good idea to describe the inner details of your place. This is because it can destroy the feeling you associate with it, or should do, of being a place that is yours and yours alone. You never have to invite or imagine any other living thing in it if you so desire, which is in effect what you are doing if you keep describing it to all you meet.

If we recall the principle of 'energy follows thought' once more we can also realise that your Sanctuary really exists, in that realm of energy so created by focussed thought. Therefore the more you visit and visualise your Sanctuary, the more real it becomes. This is a place, existing in some other dimension than the one we perceive, created by you. If you then continue to use up the energy linked to and part of your physical/imaginary Sanctuary by describing it to others, you dissipate the energy form, or gathering of energy you have worked so hard to build in your meditations. How this happens is not important, that it does is enough to remind you. It is rather like telling exam answers to others when you are the only one in the class that has bothered to learn them. Your sanctuary does not need to become a guarded castle in your mind, but it does need to remain yours, pure and unstained by the outside world, if it is to do its job successfully.

One idea that you may like to consider is making a depiction of your Sanctuary in some way. This may be by drawing it, making a collage or simply by finding a place that is similar and photographing it. You could display this in your meditation area as a reminder, not only of what your Sanctuary looks like, but to make use of it!

If your Sanctuary is a completely fictitious one, you may even one day have the most pleasant surprise of finding that it does exist somewhere in the world after all. This may not be quite as you imagine it in your meditations, but within yourself, you will know that this is the place. If so, honour it in some way, by picking up any litter there, feeding plants, cleaning or tidying in any other way and so on.

For the meditation itself, follow the same procedure in grounding and connecting as usual and then make yourself mentally ready to begin a journey. To do this, focus on the area of your forehead in the centre, where the Third Eye energy centre is located. Imagine that you are looking out at reality from within your head. Spend a little time doing this as this will adjust your level of perception to the correct and optimum level to find the best Sanctuary for you.

When you are ready, look and see that you are standing before a tall tree. This is much taller than you and is in full leaf. Look up at the topmost branches of the tree, seeing them swaying slightly in the breeze that you feel blowing across your face. This is a cooling breeze that you are glad of for beyond the tree you can see the Sun flickering behind the leaves in a cloudless and deep blue sky. The leaves and flickering sunlight dazzle you and for a moment you are entranced by them and stand staring.

Now gather your thoughts and focus on the tree once more. Slowly you follow the image of the trees down from the top. Notice the colours and patterns on the leaves and see how their stems flow into the branches and how these in turn flow into other branches. As you look your eyes are led downwards and then you are looking at the trunk of the tree, in front of you. See the patterns of the bark and if you wish reach out and feel its texture. Continue to look down and you see the roots disappearing into the Earth around your feet, below the grass that you are standing next to.

As you look around you now, you find that you are standing on a path that is laid neatly out in front of you, in a straight line. Beyond the tree there is a hedge, resplendent with colour and life. There are many berries here and flowers growing beneath the hedge. Their scent drifts up to you and you may decide to taste one of the berries. Beyond the hedge you can see a landscape of rolling hills, with a patchwork of fields. The squares of land you see are different colours with the crops growing in them, blown this way and that by the wind blowing across the hills. Some fields are bordered by other rows of hedges and here and there are small clumps of trees, with birds circling overhead in search of food. Now and again you can hear the call of a bird and also the answer echoing across the landscape.

Turn you gaze now to the other side of the path you are on and you will see that this is bordered by another hedge. This one however is too tall for you to see over and the undergrowth is so thick that you cannot see through to what is on the other side.

You begin your walk along the path now, hearing your footsteps as you go. Take your time over this, enjoying being here. You may well feel a sense of anticipation, but do not hurry, for you are in a place beyond the scope of time as we know it now. Take time to stop and smell the flowers and breathe in and taste the air here, for it is clean and good.

As you continue you can still see the rolling hills to one side but soon on the other side the hedge finishes. In its place there is a wall, again too tall for you to see over and so what is beyond, but a part of you knows that it is your Sanctuary. It is important to realise here that your Sanctuary does not have to have a brick wall inside it. Continue along the path, observing in a relaxed manner what you see and soon you come to a door in the wall.

This you know is the entrance to your Sanctuary. This may be any type of door that is closed at present. Beyond lies your Sanctuary but for now you must find the key. This is done by simply looking for it. Look around you and you will find it. It may be on the ground beside you, on the ledge in the wall, hanging next to the door, on the branch of a nearby tree or already in your pocket. If you cannot find your key this time, then return back along your path to the tree where you began and then back from your meditation. This indicates that there is something within you blocking you allowing yourself to find the rest of your Sanctuary. Meditate on what this may be and then try again.

When you have found your key, place it in the lock and turn it to open the door. Hear the lock slide smoothly back and when you are ready step through. Before looking, turn and close the door quietly behind you. Now take time, as long as you feel you need and feel comfortable with, to explore your Sanctuary. Walk around and move through your Sanctuary, seeing what you can find and making yourself familiar with it. You may not need to do anything with your Sanctuary on your first visit, but on subsequent ones you can make changes, find a place to sit for rest and contemplation and so on. For the first time, it is enough to see what you can see, to spend time wandering and creating your Sanctuary to be the most perfect place for you that you can possibly imagine. Remember that you are not limited by money or logic and in fact only by your imagination.

When you have wandered enough and feel ready, find your way back to the door where you came in. Take a last look around at your Sanctuary to remember what it is like when you return and when you feel ready, open the door and step outside once more. Turn and close the door and turn the key in the lock. Hear this slide home and then place the key where you wish. Know that it is only yourself who knows where this is kept and that your Sanctuary will remain just as it is until you return. You can return whenever you wish but for now it is time to leave. Bring with you the awareness of your Sanctuary and any experiences you may have had and return refreshed and renewed along the path.

Come back past the wall and the hedges now and soon you find that you are back at the tree where you began. Now take a seat at the base of the tree. Lean your back against its trunk and allow the tree to take your weight. As you do so you find that the tree is a perfect fit to your shape and so you relax deeply, close your eyes and let this place fade away from you.

Now make a return in the usual way, letting that other world fade away and becoming instead aware of the everyday world and place about you. Focus on your body and your breathing and return slowly and fully. Ground yourself completely as it is surprising the depths you can go to, even on the first journey. It is also a good idea to make a few brief notes when you have returned, to keep track of how your Sanctuary evolves and changes in future meditations, as it is for all that you perform.

The technique for the Sanctuary is as follows:

Ground and connect
Focus on the third eye
Journey along path to door in the wall
Visit to sanctuary
Return back along path to tree
Rest at tree and return
Ground

Meeting Your Guide

This meditation technique follows and builds on the Sanctuary which you have established. Before progressing to this meditation it is strongly recommended that you establish a good and clear Sanctuary that you can visit without too much meditational effort and one that is ideal for you. This is necessary in order to be able to pursue another level of meditation that is required for meeting your guide.

This technique is aimed at bringing about some kind of meeting with your own guide. There is a great deal of discussion and interest in guides, angels and the like at present, so this meditation is included in answer to that interest. It is NOT an attempt at defining what or who guides are, where they come from, what they do and how they do it, as this is a subject that requires a great deal more than the small Chapter I have allotted. It is a fact that humanity has made depictions of guides and angels for thousands of years, so these images must have originated somewhere, somehow. It is enough to accept that they may exist for a meeting to take place.

It may be helpful for the curious to attempt a small definition of a spiritual guide. As such I would offer 'a person, usually one who has lived previously on Earth, but who has now advanced in their development to take on the role of a non-physical entity, partly for the purpose of helping or guiding those on Earth through their lives'. This naturally brings many questions and doubtless disagreements, which I would encourage, in the hope that you would try the meditation at least a few times and let this provide you with the answers your questioning mind seeks. Again, I return to the simple and only justification I make for including this meditation: that history has shown there are beings of some kind existing beyond our everyday perception, able to assist and guide us. This meditation gives you the chance to avail yourself of this opportunity and experience what can be the most beautiful meditation.

One question, that I will endeavour to answer, and that I have found is in a great many people's minds, is why so many of these so-called guides are Tibetan monks, Native Americans and glowing robed figures. This is really quite logical, since the people in question often have lived in cultures that are or were primarily spiritual, so it is no surprise to find them progressing in this way. That said, guides do not have to be such types. They can be the smallest, scruffiest child, poorly dressed beggar and so on. You may even meet an animal (a great honour) since this means that the animal appearing to you is offering itself as a helper and frequently protector.

Should all this seem like just so much rubbish may I suggest you accept it as so and simply skip on to the next chapter. If however you are curious or unconvinced either way, please try the meditation that follows, several times, and let this 'guide' you either way.

167

It is often necessary to repeat the technique many times before a clear meeting and communication is established. To begin with you may only receive blurred or incomplete sightings or images. Please persevere with this as an adjustment needs to take place, from both sides, for the energies of each party to reach a level where they vibrate similarly and operate on the same wavelength. The process is often and accurately described as rather like tuning in a radio station. This is first focussed on the general area, establishing some kind of sound or communication and then fine-tuned, so that the words and images become clear.

To begin the technique, ground and connect in the usual way and then focus once more on the third eye energy centre, to align your awareness with the optimum energy flow to enable the higher perception necessary. Spend a little time on this, ensuring that you are in the best possible position to bring a meeting with your guide. Then take yourself on the same journey, to your Sanctuary.

Begin at the tree in the same manner as before, setting the scene and establishing it in your mind by bringing your eyes down from the tree top to the roots. Look at the hills around you, see the hedges and finally the path. Walk along the path, past both the hedges as before and alongside the wall. Take time to involve all your senses, as guides may initially communicate to you through any of them, it is common to feel a touch before any visible image is seen, or smell a fragrance first.

Move along the path to the door of your Sanctuary and pause for a moment to prepare yourself for your meeting with your guide. This is not only to remove any fear but to give yourself the correct mental attitude of expectancy and realism. When you are ready, unlock the door to your Sanctuary, open it and step inside, closing the door behind you.

Now take a few moments to walk around your Sanctuary just establishing this in your mind's eye. Then find a comfortable place to sit and await your guide. When you feel ready, always progressing in your own time, mentally request that your guide come to you in a clear image. Do this in your own way, using words that you do usually, being simple, direct, clear and polite.

Look now into the distance and you will see a glowing light, small at first but growing larger as it draws closer to you. Remain as you are, patiently watching this glowing light come to you. As you wait the light grows until it is before you. See it shimmering, perhaps one colour, perhaps many colours. Allow the light to hover where it is.

Soon you will find that your guide will appear to you. They may step clearly out of the light, or the light may dissolve to reveal them standing there. It is at this point that I leave students in silence when I am talking them through the meditation, for individual meetings to occur. Take time then to allow events to unfold. Try not to direct things with your mind, instead letting what happens and seems to want to occur, do so. This may be the unexpected, since we get the guide we deserve and need, not necessarily the one we want!

Take as long as seems necessary over this stage of the meditation. You may of course speak to your guide, possibly hearing responses in your head, as if you hear a delicate whisper, just inside your ear. You may for a time only see them, or even a part of them. There is, in most cases, a distant knowing that accompanies the guide that tells you this is precisely what they are. It may be that all you receive for now is a light touch on the face or a stroke of your hair. This may be all that is possible to begin, but this will increase and progress to a full, moving image and communication in subsequent visits.

When you have spent as long as you wish letting communication take place, know that it is time for you to leave and your guide to depart. Give them your thanks in a simple and sincere way. Always do this, even if you think nothing at all has happened, since it is impolite not to do so and guides do not take kindly to this – give them the recognition they deserve. Whilst they are never malicious, they have 'put themselves out' so to speak on your behalf and your thanks is extremely little to give them in return.

You may then see the light surround them once more and they will leave in the same manner in which they arrived. The light will drift away from you until it is but a speck and then disappears completely. It may be that you sense your guide will wait for you to depart. Whichever applies, know that you must leave now, but that you can return when you wish to communicate with your guide, when you have need.

Move back to the door of your Sanctuary and when you are ready, open it and step back on the path outside. Return the key to its usual place and walk back along the path to your tree. Return now in the usual way, taking time to ground and ensure that you return slowly and fully, bringing with you what you have experienced. Allow the place to fade away from you, feel yourself returning to your body and your surroundings. You can reach a high level of perception and awareness in this meditation, so it is doubly important to ground fully before you leave your meditation when you have done so, open your eyes.

The technique for Meeting Your Guide is as follows;

Ground and connect
Focus on third eye
Establish image of tree
Journey to sanctuary
In sanctuary, see guide coming
Communication with guide
Return to Tree
Ground

Before leaving this Chapter, I will make one brief mention of an ancient meditation method that is now universal in its application and use, but stems originally from Zen sources. The meditation technique here is to detach yourself from the ultimately limiting human view of body, mind and emotions. It is in part based on the adage that whatever we experience fully disappears. As such it is necessary to focus precisely on those things that we wish to detach ourselves from. This can lead to some startling results in heightened awareness and even revelation as to who and what we are. This is different for each individual and the effort and concentration required for this advanced technique will repay itself eventually!

The technique is to focus on the following, with my added recommendation of grounding and connecting first. Focus on the thought that you are not your body. Since you have a body and are able to feel it, you are therefore not your body. Let this awareness and consciousness settle in your mind then continue. This time concentrate on your feelings. Since you have feelings, both good and bad and are able to feel them, you are separate from them.

Now move on to your thoughts. Since you have thoughts, that come and go from your consciousness, you can observe them as they do so. Therefore, you are not your thoughts. Repeat these words to yourself, letting their meaning become clear to you and then just see where it takes you, letting yourself exist in whatever you decide is left. This may seem like a strange exercise to be doing, but can be surprising in its effect.

Though this may seem like very little to base a full and deep meditation on, which it certainly is, it is precisely this that makes it so deep. It is therefore best viewed as an advanced meditation and left until a good degree of meditative concentration is established and natural for you. This is also the case for the meditations that follow.

Chapter 9 – Advanced Meditations

We have made a journey through the wonderful landscape that is your being and have seen, learnt and dealt with much. It is hoped that by this stage of the book you have established a regular meditation practice as part of your life. Not as an extra interest or something that is additional to your daily activity, but as an integral part of its structure and format. The aim here is for meditation to be a part of you, so that you are not setting aside time for its practice so much as including it within your lifestyle. Meditation ideally becomes a part of you and you a part of your meditation, the one complementing the other.

As such it is important for your meditations to be kept alive and not be allowed to fall into a dull and lifeless habit that becomes an automatic procedure each day. It is perhaps the ideal, but nonetheless achievable goal, that you have a daily practice of meditation, to keep you in close contact with the underlying energies affecting and shaping you and your life, giving you a greater degree of awareness and so control over them. In this way meditation can go a long way to shaping the very structure of you and your life. It is also recommended that you take one day off per week, at this level, in order for those energies to recharge and to give the deeper and higher levels of your being, which you will by now be contacting on a regular basis through your meditation, a chance to rest from this new onslaught of activity. You need always to be gentle with yourself, treating yourself with as much care and attention as that given a new born baby.

In order to allow for as much progression as possible to take place in your meditational development and to encourage you to continue, I include now a selection of more advanced techniques, as guided visualisation journeys. These meditations will also ensure that there is a healthy variety to your meditation diet, so keeping at bay the slovenliness of repetition. They can also be performed at regular intervals as they provide and excellent framework for objective awareness and analysis of how you and your life are developing. These meditations are structured in such a way that different things will be felt, seen, heard and experienced each time they are performed.

The objective awareness spoken of above is also required and necessary in your interpretation of what you experience. The best person to do this is you, for it is only you that knows truly how you feel about the symbols that you see. It is important to view the content of your meditations as symbolic representations, and not literal images, of the different aspects of your being. Whilst it can be helpful for you to discuss your images with a tutor or close friend, they should only reflect what you say, not inform you of what they mean. No one knows you like you know yourself, so be honest, gentle and true. If you allow it to, your mind will capitalise on the opportunity you are giving it with the series of meditations of teaching you what it knows.

Each of the meditations that follows is a guided journey, forming part of a complete set. It is therefore suggested that you take a period of time, however long seems appropriate to you and you consider the correct number of repetitions of each, to work through your whole being in this way. Each meditation takes you to a place that as a whole is a reflection of your total self, on all its different levels.

This takes the form of a large or stately house, somewhere that most of us would like to live, if we could but do so. The type and style of building is entirely up to you and can be predetermined or spontaneous, as you decide appeals. Should you choose to predetermine the house, do allow for unexpected and differing images to those you expect to occur when you perform each meditation as you must allow time and space for those deeper and higher levels of yourself to communicate with you, as is the intention here. You must be truthful to yourself and honest. Each journey then takes you to a different room in your house, where you are able to realise information about the particular aspect of your being that the room represents. Each room is explained in the text for each meditation, with the abbreviated technique for all these meditations given as one at the end.

The meditations are more advanced in that they require a greater degree of awareness from you, as the actual image you are directed to see is only loosely described, allowing your own deeper mind to 'fill in the blanks' for you. This needs particularly to be the case when you enter the actual room that is the focus of each meditation. Here no detail is given, allowing the details to be made completely by you. By allowing spontaneous images to occur, a high degree of therapeutic knowledge can come to you, in symbolic form that can shed a great deal of light on that aspect of your being.

The Perfect Reflection

This meditation is a safe and effective means by which to discover and experience your true self and find out who you really are in your ideal state. This can be as you would wish yourself to be or as you truly are in the spiritual sense. You should decide which of these two images you want to see before beginning the meditation. Begin by grounding and connecting and experiencing the sense of balance and security that lies at the very heart of your being. Let yourself be fully aware of this, as it is this that gives you the ability to be objective and to feel safe with what you experience in the coming meditation.

You begin a journey then, visualising in the usual manner, imagining that you are looking out from within a Third Eye at the centre of your forehead. This Third Eye can see more clearly and accurately than your physical eyes. As you look, you will see that you are standing outside a large and stately house. You are standing upon a gravel driveway, with neatly trimmed edges leading into a lawn that sweeps away behind you, where you can just see some gates that are the entrance to this place. The gates are closed, as are the front doors to this beautiful house.

Take a little time now to view your house from the outside, noticing its shape, colour and condition. Allow it to form itself, without prompting from you. It may seem as if it has been preserved for many, many years and is in perfect condition. It may however, be ramshackle and run down. Whichever, pause for a moment now to reflect on what you see and to consider what this may show you about yourself, at this time.

Around, you can hear the sound of crows from nearby trees. In the corner of the drive there is large and expensive car parked. Walk over to this. When you are close enough look at the registration of the car. You will see that this is formed by the initials of your name and it is then that you realise that the car and the house it is beside, belongs to you and indeed, is you.

With this realisation, find your way to the front door of the property and enter. The doors open easily and smoothly. Once inside you are presented with a scene of a most beautiful and ideal house for you. You are in the entrance hall and can see a staircase leading up before you and doors to many rooms around you. As you look around the scene, acclimatising yourself to where you are, one door seems to be more familiar to you than the others. This may be because it is painted a different colour, made of different wood or any other reason. Move over to that door now, which is shut.

This whole place looks very familiar to you somehow and you feel as if you know it very well. When you reach the door, you find that you are able to open it easily. Enter and close the door behind you. Inside the room there is no furniture and the curtains are closed. There is enough light coming through them however for you to see. The only thing in the room is a large mirror, just taller than you. This is in the centre of the room facing you. It has its own stand and its surface is perfectly clear and clean. Move closer to the mirror and you will see that its frame is of very old and ornately carved wood, lovingly polished. Look into the mirror now and you will see that it reflects back to you the perfect image of yourself, that you have chosen to see. Here you will see yourself as you truly are, having reached and achieved the highest possibilities of your potential, either in this lifetime or throughout all your lives. Spend time now looking at and conversing with your perfect reflection. You will find that the reflection is able to answer all your questions. Take as long as you need for this.

When you have finished be sure to thank your reflection for what it has told you and shared with you. Turn away from the mirror then and find your way back to the door of this room. Open it and step back into the entrance hall of this grand place. You may perhaps wonder what lies beyond the other doors you can see, but these are for another time. Now you must leave, so walk back to the front door and step outside, closing the door behind you. You emerge into the fresh air of the place where you are able to consider what you have seen and learnt.

Walk back over to the place where you began your journey to your house, hearing your footsteps crunch the gravel once more. As you do so, there is a sound from nearby and as you look up you see an old gardener who touches his cap as you approach. You may not know who this person is, or you may have a sense of recognition and familiarity towards them. They however, seem to know you and speak to you giving you some message that may mean something to you.

Thank the gardener for his words and then continue on your way. Come back to where you began. From here let this place fade from you and return, slowly, gently and fully to your everyday level of consciousness. Bring your attention back to the centre of your being, and then to your breath. Deepen the level of your breathing and return this to its everyday level for you. Ground yourself and when you are ready, open your eyes.

The Attic Room

This meditation follows on from the Perfect Reflection, visiting again the house that functions as the structure of your own being. This time we ascend to the very top of the house, to a small and secret attic which only you know exists and contains something of the very highest aspect of your existence. This is the state of condition of your spiritual self, at the time of the meditation. You may even meet a guide or helper there.

Begin the meditation then by grounding and connecting. Imagine then that you are looking out from within, using your inner eyes or Third Eye that can see more clearly than your physical eyes. Begin to see yourself then standing once more on the gravel driveway before the house that you know now belongs to you. See the lawns sweeping away from the house, with the neatly trimmed edges and ornate bushes and hedges. In the distance you may see an apple orchard and even catch a slight scent from the herb garden and hear the buzzing of bees from the hives nearby. Walk over to the car, which remains in the driveway, noticing again the number plate.

Look again at the house and begin to move towards it, hearing your feet crunch on the gravel. As you look at the door, getting larger as you draw nearer, be aware of how you feel at being in this place once more, perhaps noticing a sense of anticipation, maybe tinged with a slight apprehension. Continue your walk to the door of your house as you do this.

Push the door open then step inside, into the cool interior. You can again see the many rooms leading off the wide entrance hall that you are in and see the wide sweeping staircase ahead of you. You begin to climb these, alone in the house yet perfectly comfortable. Soon you reach a landing, with a hallway leading away from you and other doors, all closed, to either side of it. You turn now and see the next flight of stairs ahead of you and begin to climb them, perhaps holding on to the mahogany bannisters for extra pull and support. Your footsteps echo as you climb and soon you are on the first floor of the house. Here there are carpets on the floors and a hush greets you. You move along the corridor, seeing more doors, which are closed to you for now.

A little way along this corridor you can see a smaller staircase, heading up into a darker place that you cannot make out from your position. Your curiosity aroused now, you move up these bare stone steps, treading carefully as your eyes adjust to the dimmer light here. The staircase is quite steep and becomes narrower, as you climb. The roof slopes down towards you now and you have to bend low to continue. Just as you think you will not be able to squeeze through any further, the steps finish and there is a small wooden, curved door before you that is shut. You can see an old key in an iron lock however and you are just able to turn it, the lock finally falling open with a final effort from you to turn it. You push the door open then and it creaks and scrapes the floor beneath.

Step inside then and explore what is in this room that represents the very highest aspects of yourself and your maximum potential. Spend time looking and exploring. Look at the view outside as well as what is inside, for as long as you wish. You may see objects, furniture or perhaps meet somebody while you are there. Be aware as you explore of how you feel while you are in this hidden room, that you know has never been seen by anyone before and has been kept until this time for your visit.

Soon the time comes for you to return from this enchanting and interesting place. Now you have discovered it however, you are able to return whenever you wish to learn and discover more. Find your way back to the door and step back out to the top of the staircase. Close the door and turn the creaky key so the door is locked. Tread carefully back down the stairs, stretching up as you are able and seeing the brighter lights of the top floor of the house as you descend. Come back along the corridor and then descend the wide flat of the stairs down to the entrance hall. Find yourself back then at the door of the house and step back out into the open air.

The light has faded now and it is early evening. You may like to stand and reflect a little, perhaps even seeing a small window tucked away at the top of the house that you know is your attic room. As you stand to look, there is the quiet sound of footsteps drawing close to you across the gravel and you hear the voice of the gardener once more, greeting you. As you turn to look at him he touches his cap again and you can just make out the words he mumbles to you, which may mean something to you in this meditation. Thank him for his words, whether you understand them or not and make your way back to your starting point. When you are ready make your return in the usual way, bringing with you what you have learnt, ensuring that you ground fully.

The Kitchen

This meditation continues with the journey through the house we have created before which serves to represent the functioning of yourself, on many different levels and from many different aspects. This time we make a journey to the kitchen of the house, which represents the mental, planning and logical aspect of yourself.

Begin this meditation then by relaxing and sinking into yourself to feel the place of balance and peace at the centre of your being. Feel yourself as grounded below and connected above and allow yourself to be guided through this journey. As you look out from within you will see that you are standing on the gravel driveway, bordered as before by the neatly trimmed edges of an immaculate lawn.

Look around you and see your very own stately house before you, tall and majestic, perfectly preserved in every way, yet with an air of time and mystery about it. Parked to one side of the driveway is your car, large and expensive, with your own name as its number plate. Move over to the large entrance doors of the house, hearing your footsteps crunch the gravel as you go.

When you reach the doors see their detail before you clearly and when you feel ready to, open them. Once inside you can see the large entrance hallway clearly, with antique tables decorated by statues and objects, some of which may be familiar to you. The staircase sweeps grandly up before you, but this time you do not climb the stairs. Instead you follow the thickly carpeted hallway alongside the stairs, moving towards the back of the house. You pass by many doors to the left and right as you go, perhaps making a mental note to explore one or two that may seem to stand out to you as you go.

Soon you reach a door at the end of the hallway. From here many smells and fragrances rise up to greet you and driven forward by these you open the door. You enter into your kitchen. This is a kitchen where much is happening although on one is here at present. Many articles are placed as if they have been in use and just left. Perhaps there are things cooking, or in preparation. Take time now to look around your own kitchen, seeing what you can find. Explore cupboards and drawers, see what is being prepared and remember to be aware of how you feel about this place. Take as long as you need now.

When you have examined this room to your satisfaction, find your way back to the door and step back into the hallway. As you walk slowly back along the hall, deep in thought, you realise that the kitchen is a place that represents your thoughts and what is affecting your mind at present. Take your time returning to the entrance hall so that you can learn from what you see. Come back outside and turn and look at the house.

Take a moment or two now to settle this image in your mind, enjoying the benefit and knowledge this place is giving you. Then you hear the sounds of the gardener approaching and you turn to meet him. He touches his cap as before and you hear the words of his message to you at this time. Thank him and make your way back then to where you began. From here let the house and place you are in fade from view when you are ready and then make your return, gently and slowly, ensuring your senses are back to their everyday feel before you open your eyes.

The Cellar

In the next of our series of Meditations through your own stately home we come to explore the cellar. As before the meditation takes the form of a guided journey through a stately home that is a symbolic representation of your inner self, on different levels as represented by the different rooms you explore. Here we descend to the cellar of your house, which reflects the deepest level of your being, that which you have buried or forgotten. This can be a place of remarkable insight and valuable information, it can however be a little reluctant to emerge, so be patient and gentle in your journeys to this room, returning as often as you need.

Begin the meditation then by grounding and connecting yourself in the usual manner and experiencing the balance at the centre of your own being. This is important as it allows for you to be objective and honest in what you experience. When you are ready begin to visualise, imagining that you look out from within, through a third eye that sees truthfully and clearly.

As you look, you find that you are back on the gravel driveway leading up to your own magnificent stately home. Look around you and become acclimatised to what you can see. Notice the gardens of the home, the trees, the air, the temperature and anything else that may be there. Begin to walk towards the home, drawing nearer with excitement and pleasure at being here once more. Your house begins to be familiar and comfortable now.

Then move on to the home itself. Parked near to the doors is a large expensive car. Walk up to this and look inside and around it.

Notice that the number plate is your name. How does this make you feel?

When you are ready then, step up to the doors and open them finding they open easily. Move inside to the entrance hall and become accustomed to what you see. As you look you see that there is a flight of stairs leading off to one side, going down, to what you know is the servants' quarters. Climb down these stairs, treading carefully as you go. As you go down you find that the light becomes darker and darker and you pause whilst your eyes adjust. When you reach the bottom of the stairs, there is a door that is closed, which you can just make out before you. Try the door. If it opens, you may enter, perhaps with some difficult. If it does not retrace your steps outside and leave the meditation for it is not yet time for you to explore what is down there (you may like to consider why this is so). If your door opens simply step inside and take as long as you wish to explore and consider what you find there.

When you are ready and feel it is time, find your way back to the door and step through, closing it behind you. Climb the stairs again and bring with you what you have learnt and experienced. Find your way back then to the front doors of your house and step back outside. Go across the driveway once more and stand and look at your home. It is then that the gardener pays his now customary visit to you, giving you a message that is relevant to the journey you have just made and to that aspect of yourself.

Return now to your starting place and begin to let the house fade away from you, returning to the everyday world around you, until the time of your next visit. Ground fully and open your eyes when you are ready.

The cellar represents that part of ourselves which we often wish to bury. It may contain relics and symbols of things you have buried from your everyday life, unconscious memories that can actually teach you much, and fears that limit or threaten you. It is the very deepest level of your being from which you can learn much.

The Dining Room

Here we explore the dining room of your stately house as the image of your being. This part of your house and self relates to and symbolises your practical nature and the structure of your life.

Begin with your grounding and connecting and then begin your inner journey, looking out from within at the level of your third eye, knowing that this will show you truth. As you look you find yourself standing back on the gravelly driveway before your own large and stately home. You walk towards the front doors, becoming accustomed to your surroundings. Hear the noise of birds in the trees lining the driveway. Look out across your grounds. Come to see a large and expensive car parked beside the door and see that the number plate is yours.

When you are ready walk up steps to your front door and enter, finding the doors unlocked. You find yourself then in the entrance hall, with the wide sweeping staircase before you and hallways leading off to other rooms. All the doors that you can see are closed. You walk down one hallway now, with thick, plush carpet covering it. Soon you come to a polished wooden door, beyond which you know lies the dining room.

Pause if you feel the need to gather yourself and your awareness and enter when you are ready. Explore this room now, in your own time and in your own way. Are you alone there? Is there everything neat and tidy or very haphazard and messy? What is the condition of the décor in the room like? Is there a pleasant atmosphere, is it stuffy and dark or light and airy? Is a meal prepared or is there a bare table? Walk around the room, changing anything you wish and doing anything you wish. Explore your room for as long as you like.

When you are ready, come back to the door and step outside to the hallway, knowing that you can return any time you wish, as it is your house. Walk back along the hall to the entrance and then go back outside, closing the front doors behind you. As you walk back across the driveway you come across the old man tending the garden.

You pause to greet him and fin that he has a message for you, relevant to your meditation. Listen to this, thank him and then walk over to where you began your journey here. When you are ready let the place fade away and make your return in the usual manner, ensuring that you have returned fully and completely.

The condition of your dining room will tell you much about your practical life and how organised you are being at the time you perform this meditation. Be aware when you have returned what your room may have been telling you about the structure of your everyday life.

The Bedroom

We now come to the bedroom within the being of your stately home. Perhaps predictably the journey here concerns your sensual self, your sexuality, as well as your need for relaxation. What you experience in the bedroom in this meditation will therefore reflect the condition and how you relate to this aspect of yourself, at this time.

Begin in the usual manner with grounding and connecting and from the third eye contact progress to the visualisation of the house. See yourself on the gravel driveway in the immaculate grounds and spend a little time establishing the image and setting the scene so that it becomes real to you. Walk over to the car then and proceed to the doors. Enter your house and then climb the carpeted stairs. Walk down a hallway in front of you, following your intuitive lead, to where you know your bedroom is.

The door is closed when you get there, but opens easily when you try. Step inside and spend time exploring, Notice the décor, its condition and colour. Is the room tidy and has it been given attention recently or does it show signs of being ignored or neglected? Is your inclination to rest and sleep or pursue some other activity! Notice the atmosphere of your room too, sensing if this is relaxing and easy for you, or perhaps makes you feel a little uncomfortable. Do you feel at ease being here and can you see details in the room clearly? What action might you take to bring about more comfort here and make it more open to others, if you wish?

When you have spent as long as you feel you need in the bedroom of the house come back to the door and step outside to the hallway again. Move back down the stairs to the front door of the house and step back outside. As you walk across the driveway you hear the gardener approach. Stop to greet him, see him touch his cap and listen for his words relating to your meditation. Thank him and leave, walking back to where you began.

From here allow the place to fade from view until your next visit. Make certain that you return slowly and fully, grounding yourself in the usual way before opening your eyes.

The Study

The Study, or library, of your house will show you details and aspects of your developing self, what you are learning from in your life at this time and what you are working on in your overall progression. This meditation can offer a great opportunity for increasing your awareness of how you are evolving and if you are learning the correct lessons necessary for this to occur.

The meditation begins with grounding and connecting and next the attunement and focussing in your third eye energy centre. From here visualise your house as before and walk over to the front doors, seeing your car still parked in the driveway. Enter inside the house, which should by now feel pleasant, comfortable and familiar to you.

This time you remain on the ground floor and follow a hallway towards the back of the house. Notice what you see en route to the study, located in a quiet corner at the back of the building as this may give you some extra information, also in pictures on the walls, colours painted there and so on.

When you reach the end of the hallway, you reach a small closed door, marked 'Study'. Open the door quietly and bending a little, enter. Now take time to walk around the room, perhaps sit at a desk and look from there and just do as you please. Notice again the condition of the room, its usefulness and practicality, as this will reflect if you are working efficiently or haphazardly in your life. You may choose to select a book from the many that line the shelves. If you open his you may read some lines, see an image or just one word that will have some relevance to you. Spend as long as you like here, observing and learning.

Now find your way back to the door and bend again to walk out to the hallway. Knowing you can return when you like, retrace your steps to the front doors and step back outside. Cross the driveway and find a quiet spot to sit and reflect on what you have seen and perhaps to determine on a future action or direction it seems appropriate to take. As you do so, the gardener approaches and gives you some words of encouragement or meaning, to help you.

Thank him and then just let the place fade from your inner vision, becoming aware instead of your breath. Deepen this and ground as usual, ensuring your full and safe return before moving.

The Locked Room

This last meditation offers a slightly different approach to learning from the symbolic representation of your being that is your stately house. The journey is designed to enable you to discover a piece of information that you have prevented yourself from knowing or accessing for some reason. It could even be a piece of higher guidance or wisdom that you receive. This may be applicable personally to you or may take the form of an insight useful for many people to know. Simply follow the meditation through and see what information, realisation or awareness comes to you that you have not considered before, or have forgotten. One tip here, is not to try to get a realisation or nugget of wisdom. Be true and if you receive nothing, do not despair. Simply leave and return another time, building the structure of this room more and more, as well as your patience, and at some stage, something will come to you.

The meditation begins as before with the customary grounding and connecting and then focussing on the third eye to allow for correct and true images and realisations to occur. See your house clearly and walk from the grounds across the driveway to the front doors, passing your car as you go. Climb the steps to the front door and enter.

From this stage of the journey you are on your own. You are looking now for a key, that is special in some way – you will know how and that it is the correct key when you find it. It can only be found by intuition and really by it finding you. Walk in whichever direction seems correct to you, observing carefully and proceeding slowly, to ensure you do not begin to apply logic and so miss your key.

Wander about until you either run out of patience and return or find the key. No other alternatives are open to you in this meditation. When you have found the key, you must then find the correct room that the key will allow you access to. Again, this can only be found by intuition and so you must allow this to take you in the direction you sense is right until it is found. Once this has been done, unlock the door and enter the room, closing the door behind you.

Spend time now in this room, in whatever way seems appropriate. There may be nothing in the room, in which case you must wait until something occurs, or someone might arrive to speak with you. You may just be required to be there for a time, without any conscious thought at all. There may perhaps be a chair or a desk for you to sit in or at and to proceed from there. By now you should be advanced enough to direct your own meditation, by allowing to occur what seems to want to, taking a back seat with your conscious and logical mind and letting it lead you where it will.

Spend as long as is necessary in this room, whatever may happen there, and when you are ready step back outside, closing and being careful to lock, the door behind you. Leave the key in the lock as in order for you to find it in the same way as before, it will be removed for you and placed in another place than where it was originally found.

You can now return, leaving the house and stepping across to a comfortable area to sit and rest, bringing with you and reflecting on what you have realised. There is no gardener in sight this time, as he can add nothing to the pure insight you have realised. When you feel ready, let the house fade away and make a return in the usual manner. Return particularly slowly from this journey as it can have the effect of taking you to a deep level. As such it is easy to lose some content of what you have learnt, however aware you may think you are of it during meditation. Just like dreams, we are returning from another world when we return from meditation and must do so gently and gradually lest the shift is too drastic for us to hold on to what is valuable from the otherworld. Ground fully then and open your eyes when you are ready.

The techniques for the stately home meditation are as follows:

Ground and connect
Adjust and attune to third eye
Visualise stately house and car with registration plate
Find particular room for your journey

188

Spend time in room, following intuitive responses
Return from room, outside to grounds
Receive message or words from gardener
Give thanks and allow house to fade
Ground

The meditations given above are really just a selection of those possible from the structure and framework that the stately home format gives us. There are many rooms possible within such a structure that only your imagination applies limits to, from where you may visit and what you may learn. Some suggestions for other rooms to visit and how they apply to aspects of your being could be:

A garage, to see by what method you travel and move through your life and how its mechanics operate – smoothly or otherwise.

A spare room, to see what untapped potential is stored within your being that you have not yet accessed, or alternatively to see what you have forgotten, left behind or are ignoring that can be of use to you.

A bathroom, where you can envisage and see what aspects of yourself you are wasting, or what is in need of cleansing and healing.

A lounge, where the only purpose is to rest and recover.

You are quite at liberty to add to this list or to decide on alternative representations of your room, as you decide applies. Stick to the same format and structure for your meditations however as the familiarity already established will go a long way to giving you clear images and so raising your confidence when embarking on your own meditations for the first time.

Chapter 10..........And Relax!

We have travelled through a rich and varied landscape, within and without your being and I trust, have learnt and discovered a great deal. It has been my hope through this book, to set those who have been mistrustful or ignorant, on a path of meditation that will enrich and bestow control and productivity to their lives. It can only be a hope and nothing more, since these things cannot be manufactured by me or any other, including yourself.

They must instead be nurtured, lovingly cared for and fed a daily diet that will result in a strong, flowering growth of self. The eventual aim is to produce a self that is aware, awake, in control of its direction and reason, able to move steadily through one's life facing disaster, triumph, joy and sadness with equal measure and celebration. This does not have to be a withdrawal from extremes of emotion, though this more traditional Eastern approach is perfectly valid and effective. It may be that our Western minds, bodies, lives and society are so enmeshed in a mass of whirling detail that is near to impossible to detach oneself fully from such extremes.

Here we can apply a principle we have met before, that which states that whatever we experience completely, disappears. Thus, by being open and embracing our society, with all its venom, prejudice, misguided ethics and practices, we can seek to transcend and transform it. This we do by transcending and transforming ourselves. This is not to suggest that we must embrace the fullness of society by becoming a respectable law abiding person society, doing only what is acceptable all the time and letting full free thinking go. Instead quite the opposite!

Here we can apply a principle we have met before, that which states that whatever we experience completely, disappears. Thus, by being open and embracing our society, with all its venom, prejudice, misguided ethics and practices, we can seek to transcend and transform it. This we do by transcending and transforming ourselves. This is not to suggest that we must embrace the fullness of society by becoming a respectable, law abiding person society, doing only what is acceptable all the time and letting full free thinking go. Instead quite the opposite!

The accomplished use of the underlying energy that we have learnt from the meditations in this book produce a responsibility that arises with full awareness of who and what you are. This responsibility, in each individual across the world is what must be sought, if we are to rise above the traps and limits of mundane life of mere existence and mediocrity.

As such, anarchy, in the true meaning of the word as self-responsibility, a state of lawlessness, because no such limiting laws are needed for the governing of the self, is required. A daily practice of meditation that induces such control becomes the norm within our lives and not a detachment. Seek to include, not to separate.

By embracing all that society, ourselves and other individuals that constitute it, contains, so we are set free from it. It is in this way that we can fulfil the old adage of being in this world but not of it. Rather than seeing all that is negative, all that is destroying the world and its unique beauty, focus on that which is rebuilding it, that which is beautiful and good. In this way you will attract those beings and circumstances to you that reflect this, as opposed to continually finding that you meet people who use and abuse you, and experiences that bring you down and threaten your progress and development. You are in control and only you can do something about your life. Meditation is a gentle, safe, effective and entirely beneficial way to achieve these things.

It has been my experience that the world is full of disaster, pain, prejudice and unspiritual activity. It has also been my experience that meditation allows for a view of this world that is beautiful and awe inspiring. Meditation also provides for me the very thing that, in all truth, keeps me alive. The reason that I can see a beauty in a world that rapes, destroys, is unfair and in many ways evil, is from the sense of the sacred that meditation gives me.

This sense of the sacred, however it is expressed, is vital to my continuing life, vital to life itself and brings hope, trust, faith, belief, vision and progression. Whilst this is a book that attempts to set up a practical approach and practice of meditation, I have to admit to another, more discreet hope, that meditation will result in a flowering of this sense of the sacred in those that read it. Notice from the positive list given above that all these things are intangible and that it is vital to realise you must also act on the fruits that your meditations give.

In this way the world becomes a little more optimistic. Amidst all the pain, we can feel love. There may seem at times no point in this, for all around is this doom and destruction. But no point is required. Adhere to the philosophy of being a 'pointless optimist' and you create an indestructible building, beautiful and limitless, and you create an indestructible building, beautiful and limitless, within your mind, body and spirit that can truly change the world. Many things are required to build this structure, meditation being the foundation and cornerstone.

In closing then, I would encourage you to complete that building, adding to your daily practice of meditation with the bricks and cement that binds it all together. Such things as diet, rest, play, music and artistic stimulation are all required for the pointless optimist who sees only love and beauty in the world. They are not some soft 'hippy' however, but a being whose awareness is sharp and acute, in control, who avoids conflict and pain because it has no part of them. They are assured of these things by the sense of the sacred that pulses forever within them. If this appeals to you, begin to meditate and all else can, and will, follow.

Appendix A

The Eastern view of energy or Chi permeating all things and existing in all things is one that we utilise here. As such in the meridian system there are concentrations of energy in certain places, dependent on the individual in terms of build, emotion, mental condition and much more besides, being that which makes the individual so. As such blockages and weaknesses in the flow of energy through the body can be created by the disharmonious muscle operation, lingering emotion, and habitual negative thought and so on. By focussing a flow of pure energy force along the relevant meridian to clear the blockage or strengthen the weakness a return to health is instigated at its basic energy level.

The 'relevant meridian', is decided by its path and organs and functions to which it is linked. These are shown under the individual meditations for each meridian. As with the aura and chakra meditations, the method for each meridian meditation is the same, simply adjusting the route to fit the meridian being focussed on. The outline for the technique is therefore given at the end of all these meditations, as before.

During the meditations you may feel any of the previously described 'energy sensations', such as heat, cold, tingling etc. Remember that these are your responses to the energy, not the energy itself. What you sense and how you feel during the meditation, may give you some idea as to the cause of a weakness or blockage in your system. The fact that you sense anything tells you that something is happening, it not being essential to understand what this is for it to work. It will happen anyway, so long as you are able to keep your focus and concentration. Your level of concentration is in direct relation to the level, dose or quality of energy that you are able to transmit during the meditation and so the benefit you obtain from it. If you have followed the meditations in the book chronologically, practiced faithfully as you went, your concentration should have reached a good level by now.

So we have the meridian system of energy vessels through the body along which we transmit a pure healing force, from start to end. This energy flow manifests as our physical condition, having its relation emotionally, mentally and spiritually, the human system being inter-related in this way. As such these meditations can be combined with complementary treatments such as acupuncture and acupressure. These treatments place needles or fingers at specific points along the meridians to instigate the flow of energy along them. As such to introduce a meditative concentration to the flow being treated at the time, significantly increases the effect. Be gentle with yourself however, for a uniform, balanced concentration of energy is what is required for healthy body, mind and spirit, not a blazing volcanic lava flow!

There are twelve main or 'regular' meridian, lines throughout the body, controlling its main functions. These are grouped into six pairs, and so we have six meridian meditations that we can effectively perform here. We can now add a seventh meditation for the 'Governing' and 'Conception' meridians, whose names describe their function. For those interested and aware of such things in each pair there is a 'complementary Opposite' of one 'yin' or female, passive meridian line and one 'yang' or male and active. As such we arrive at a balanced and uniform flow of energy through our bodies in each meditation. In each meditation we begin with the Yin meridian. The meridians flow in the direction given in the meditations, needless to say.

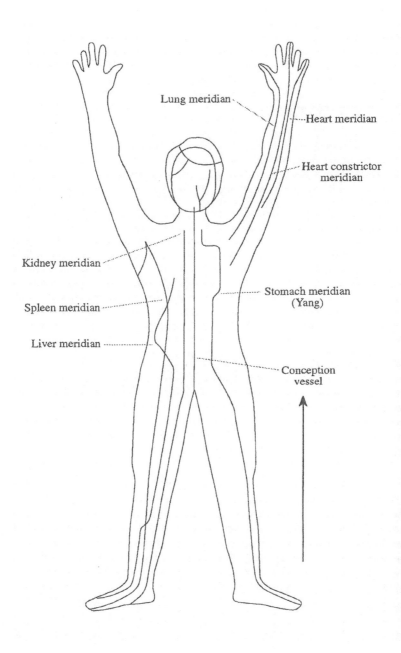

Lung meridian

Heart meridian

Heart constrictor meridian

Kidney meridian

Spleen meridian

Liver meridian

Stomach meridian (Yang)

Conception vessel

THE MERIDIAN SYSTEM – FRONT VIEW

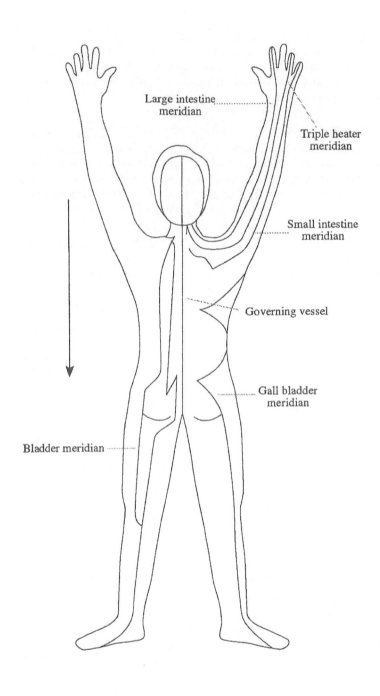

THE MERIDIAN SYSTEM – BACK VIEW

Before the meditations are given it may be of worth to give some of the main reasons for a disharmony in a meridian. These can be an incorrect diet for that individual, an allergy, worry, muscle strain, infection, incorrect job, bad posture, stress, tension, tiredness, too high or low metabolic rate, lack of or too much exercise and so on. This potentially endless list makes the point clearly for us that all things have their energy equivalent and all things are affected by this energy.

There remains one last point to make before we begin the meditations. This addresses itself to those with a deeper interest and knowledge of Chinese medicine than is the norm. In this ancient system of medicine, energy as we have come to know it is divided into five constituent parts in the body, these being Chi, Jing, Blood, Body Fluids, and Shen. For the sake of simplicity and ease I am here treating these five as one, but if you have the necessary expertise you are of course free to divide the meditations accordingly.

Experienced people may also recognise some elements of the Chinese Zang Fu system in the correspondences of the meditations with the organs they affect and are welcome to use these as they are aware. If such a person you may also like to perform the meditations at the optimum time of energy flow through the relevant organs associated with the meridians, as given below for the rest of us. For those unfamiliar with any of the organs listed below, refer to the relevant meditation for more information.

Lung	-3-5am
Large Intestine	-5-7am
Stomach	-7-9am
Spleen	-9-11am
Heart	-11am – 1pm
Small Intestine	-1-3pm
Bladder	-3-5pm
Kidney	-5-7pm

Pericardium	-7-9pm
San Jiao	-9-11pm
Gall Bladder	-11pm – 1pm
Liver	-1-3am

Lung and Large Intestine Meridian Meditation

We begin this series of meditation with the meridian that travels through and is therefore linked with the Lung and Large Intestine Meridians. First a look at the function of these organs to discover what we may treat specifically with these meditations. Remember that as we are dealing with a system that is primarily Eastern in origin we take their interpretation of the function of the organs which is primarily on an energy level.

The Lungs govern the flow of Chi energy and the respiration of the body. Effective functioning of the lungs is vital to overall energy levels and the motivation and fortitude this brings. If you are a smoker, or preferably giving up, this meridian is good to focus on for meditation. The Lungs govern the inhalation of pure air and energy and the exhalation of the impure. The Lungs take energy from the spleen, as this extracts energy from the food you eat. The Lungs then distribute the resultant energy, from air and food, in whatever quality and condition, round your body. The energy from the lungs also protects against cold and damp in the body, depleting the system.

Use this meridian meditation to treat colds. Also blockages here may result in asthma, coughs and breathing problems. Swelling in the face is also an indication of impute lung energy. Since the lung energy regulates the movement of bodily fluids, urine retention, poor hair and skin condition (dry or excessively sweaty) are indicators that all is not well here. A poor sense of smell is another factor to be considered.

On a different level, if you are excessively sad or stricken with grief, for whatever reason, this affects the lungs and their energy flow. You may like to help yourself overcome this state by using this meditation. The Lungs also give us a sense of belonging and connection to the rest of the world: feeling a part of all things, as we truly are. Use this meditation if you are truly alone and wish to belong.

Signs to look out for are shortness of breath, a weak voice, pale face, tiredness, lethargy and sweating. This meditation is particularly good for those who work in offices, as the bad posture this demands results in a lung energy deficiency. If you have taken antibiotics recently, it is also good to stimulate the lung energy flow that they can impair, with this meditation.

Moving on to the Large Intestine Meridian, we now examine its energy effects. It is important to realise that since the two are paired, those attributes or deficiencies given for the Lungs also apply for the Large Intestine (and also for the other Meridians so paired for the meditations). Specifically the Large Intestine receives that which is impure from the small intestine, extracts what is pure and excretes the rest. If you live or work in a polluted environment, this is a good meditation to use. If you have a poisoned system, use this meditation (the first meditation hangover cure!). Any problems with the colon or excretory system can also be helped here.

For the meditation itself, firstly perform your grounding and connecting. This is essential here as it is necessary to have the subtle awareness this brings, so as to sense the movement and reaction you have to the energy flow stimulated by your thoughts. Take a moment to bring to mind those specific problems, if any, you are treating and then begin. Focus your concentration on a point in your body on the right shoulder at the front, in the hollow beneath the collar bone. Spend a little just establishing this point and in your mind and imagining a small sphere of energy forming here.

This should be a crystal clear, pure ball of energy, the most pure force of life that you can possibly imagine.

When you are ready, begin to move this sphere of energy along the path of the lung meridian. Move at a comfortable pace for you. Try to allow the energy sphere to move at its own pace, for it will sense blockages and weaknesses as it foes and adjust itself accordingly. This is because your subconscious knows where it needs energy and will absorb this at the relevant places. Therefore try to get your mind out of the way, just observing what happens as the energy sphere moves through your body.

Remain relaxed, still and observant. If you sense that the meridian is blocked simply focus a concentration of energy to the sphere, which gently smooths it away and then continues on its journey. Continue in this manner until you have reached the end of the meridian. Repeat the movement if you feel it necessary, being gentle and aware as you go. You may also find it difficult to concentrate at certain points, which is another indication of a blockage. Redouble your efforts to concentrate and repeat the unblocking method above and continue.

For the lung meridian then move from that point in your chest up an inch or so and then out to your shoulder, moving the energy sphere just beneath your shoulder bone.

Now bring your focus down your right arm, moving down the inside of the arm, near the uppermost surface, but inside. Continue slowly and gently down over your wrist and out to the end of your thumb.

Pause for a moment and be aware of what effect this energy movement has had upon you and be aware of anything you have realised now. Now repeat the lung meridian movement on the left side, following the same path on the opposite side of your body.

When this has been done, pause a little as above and then begin the Large Intestine Meridian energy cleansing.

This begins at the tip of your first finger and moves through your hand, over its back and gently to a point on your wrist. The large intestine meridian then moves up in a gentle curve towards the back of your arm, to your elbow. From here the curve is repeated, moving up in the same arc to a point above the back of your armpit. From here focus the energy sphere moving across the back of your shoulder to your neck. The meridian line then moves up through your neck, beneath your ear and across your face to the side of the top of your upper lip, where it ends.

This path must be repeated on both sides of the body, moving firstly up through your right arm and then your left, performing the exercise in exactly the same way for each side.

Remember to smooth out any blockages and to focus a stronger flow of concentration of energy where you sense any weaknesses. Move in your own time and when you have finished pause and allow awareness to come to you of the difference this has made to you, physically, mentally, emotionally and spiritually. Then ground again and return.

Spleen Meridian and Stomach Meridian Meditation

The second meridian meditation is that which is linked to the spleen and stomach. Taking the spleen first, it is viewed as governing the bodies' abilities of transportation and transformation. The spleen is the main organ of digestion, so any digestive disorders can be helped with this meditation. As previously mentioned, the spleen extracts positive energy from the food in your stomach and sends this to the lungs and heart, where it is transformed into Chi energy and blood. If you have a poor appetite, poor digestion or diarrhoea, use this meditation.

The Spleen also regulates the flow of blood through the vessels. Any weakness here is shown as easy bruising and blood appearing in the stools. Also, if you have varicose veins, this meditation can help, with positive application of energy and thought.

Since the spleen dominates the muscles and limbs a deficiency of energy along this meridian can result in weak muscles and limbs that do not have good tone and shape. If you also have excessive tiredness, use this meditation.

Since we are concerned here with digestion, this also involves the mouth. If your sense of taste seems dull or you have mouth ulcers or dull and pale lips, this meditation can improve things here. If you find that your eating patterns are irregular, this can damage the spleen, so this meditation will help put things right.

Lastly, the spleen is considered as sending a clear energy to the head and brain. If you feel very confused, are finding that you are thinking the same thoughts over and over and cannot concentrate, focus on the flow of energy moving clearly along this meridian and it will clear any blockages you may have here. This will also increase your decisive capabilities, if you have trouble in this capacity. Equally, if you cannot switch your mind off, even after meditation, this technique can help to clear your head to allow this to occur. This will clear any pensiveness you may have.

For the stomach, we focus our attention, perhaps predictably on the role of receiving and storing food. Of prime importance of course is the quality and condition of the food you give to your stomach, but that is a matter for others better qualified than I to preach about! If however, you find that you suffer frequently from nausea, hiccups, vomiting or belching, then this meditation may help to clear the incorrect flow of stomach energy, which will enable you to absorb your food adequately. This meridian is also linked, , via the pancreas, to the flow and amount of insulin in the blood, which means that this meditation is a good one for those diagnosed as diabetic to perform regularly.

To begin this meditation, ground and connect yourself and as before allow yourself a pause to take stock of yourself and your being. Bring to mind that which you are aware is in need of treatment or what you wish to focus upon in the meditation and then adjust your awareness to the energy and life force within your body.

Bring your point of concentration to the beginning of the spleen meridian, which is in your foot, on the top of your big toe, beginning with the right foot. Focus the clear energy sphere at this point, ensuring you are aware of this clearly before tracing the meridians path through your body. When you are ready move your energy sphere through the inside of your foot, curving up before your ankle and then running, smoothly and gently up the inside of your leg in the centre. Continue this movement to the top of your leg, unblocking any obstructions as you go and strengthening any weaknesses you may sense. When you have reached the top of your leg begin to move out in a gentle curve through your abdomen to a point just in and up an inch or two from the armpit. From here the spleen meridian moves down again to finish just below the armpit.

Allow yourself a little time to pause and rest and let your concentration gather once more. Be aware of any differences you may feel in body, mind and spirit and when you are ready, repeat the spleen meditation on the other side of the body, moving up your left leg and following the same pattern as before.

Pause again and become aware of the difference this may have made. It is vital that you are consciously aware of the changes you have brought about to your condition with these meditations for it is precisely this change of consciousness that makes them so effective, as this constitutes a change of reality as you perceive it.

This changes how you think and, as we know, the energy of your thoughts creates the reality you experience.

When you are ready to continue, move your attention to the beginning of the stomach meridian line, to commence the cleansing here. This actually begins in two separate places. The first is on the head, to the right side, above and to the side of the right eye. Move the energy sphere down from here, curving past the eye to the side of the chin. Now refocus the sphere of crystal energy beneath your right eye and move this slowly and gently down to join the other point you have just left. Then continue on your journey, ensuring your awareness of the energy sphere is clear. Move at your own natural pace down through your neck to the collar bone. Trace the meridian right al little so that it is above your nipple. Then move clearly straight down with your visualisation over the other nipple. From here curve in slightly and move down through your body to the top of your leg. Focus the energy sphere continuing down through your right leg, through the middle and front of your right leg to our knee. At the knee cap there is a slight zig zag motion outwards and the meridian moves down closer to the outside of the lower leg as a result. Finally, bring your energy ball down to a point in the centre of the foot on the top.

Pause and rest here for a time and notice the adjustments you have made. When you are ready repeat the path of this meridian on the left side, from the head and eye down and then to your left foot. Take stock of the difference, rest a short time and ground yourself fully, bringing the benefit of the meditation to your everyday life, returning when you are ready.

Heart Meridian and Small Intestine Meridian Meditation

We come now to the meridian lines that are based around the function of the Heart and the Small Intestine. This organ is regarded as having a similar function in Chinese medicine as in

Western. It controls and regulates the flow of blood through the body's vessels. This is essential for the body's warmth, so if you suffer severely from cold or chilblains, this is a good meditation to use. Of course any conditions relating to the heart and its function will benefit from this meditation too. The same is true for any inefficiency in the blood.

He heart is considered as housing Shen in Chinese Medicine. The concept of the Shen is a complex one but is perhaps best described as that which gives our individual personality. If you feel that you lack identity, are stuck in the mass of civilisation, use this meditation. It is also said that the condition of Shen can be seen in the eyes, so put a twinkle back in your eyes with this meditation!

Other aspects covered by the Heart are the complexion and the tongue, the condition of which can be improved by clearing this meridian. Also the function of sweating, essential in any normal healthy body, is linked to the function of the Heart. If you have an imbalance here, use this meditation. This can be linked to excess or deficient heat or cold in the body.

The ability to manifest joy in a balanced way comes under this meditation, so if you feel you need more joy or perhaps are telling yourself you and your life are so happy when in fact they are not, this meditation is for you.

Signs to look out for here are an irregular pulse, cold or clammy hands, palpitations, shortness of breath and pains in the chest and even a dark red or purple looking tongue.

The function of the small intestine is to separate that which is pure from that which is impure, in the body. Specifically the small intestine receives partially digested food from the stomach. Here what is waste is passed to the Large Intestine and bladder for excretion. So any problems with this process in your body should be focussed on with this meditation.

The Heart Meridian begins in the chest, as you might expect. Begin the technique with your grounding and connecting, bringing to mind any specific condition you may be treating. When you are ready focus the energy sphere on the right side of your chest, a little above and centre from the armpit.

Spend a little time establishing the ball of energy and when you feel ready, begin to focus on its movement, slowly and naturally, down your right arm. It will travel along the inner underside of your arm, moving in a straight line to your elbow. Be aware as you go of any blockage or breaks in concentration and imagine the ball of energy spreading out and smoothing out the obstruction. From the elbow continue down the arm in the same straight line to the wrist, then flowing through the hand to the end of the little finger where it ends. Pause for a moment to take stock of the effect this has had upon you and repeat the same process, this time down your left arm, from the chest to the little finger.

Pause once more and then continue with the small intestine meridian. This begins on the outer side of the little finger of the right hand moving up through it, to the centre as it foes. From here flow up through the arm with your sphere of cleansing energy until you have reached a point midway through the shoulder. From here move back down and to the centre until you are above the armpit and centre from it. Then curve up through the neck to the right side of your face, above the chin. Lastly move back and up across your face with the energy ball until you have reached the point below the ear lobe, where the small intestine meridian finishes. Pause here and become aware of what you sense now and then repeat this procedure for the left side and arm. Move the energy ball slowly and comfortably for you, smoothing out any blockages or distractions you notice as you go. Take your time, do not rush and be aware of what is happening as you perform the meditation.

When you have moved the energy ball up to your left ear, slowly ground yourself and return, bringing back with you to ordinary reality what you have gained and benefited from in the meditation. Take time to adjust and when you are ready, open your eyes.

Kidney Meridian and Bladder Meridian Meditation

The Kidneys are viewed as having many and important functions in the system of Chinese medicine used here. This begins with the function of storing and reproducing Jing. Jing is basically viewed as the essence of life, so we can see how vital the efficient functioning is to the health of the body, as well as mind and spirit. Jing also gives your body strength and governs growth and development through childhood (making this an excellent meditation for those children able to perform it) and sexual and reproductive functioning. Any problems with retarded growth, learning difficulties, infertility and sexual problems and senility can be helped with this meridian meditation.

The Kidneys also produce marrow and manufacture blood. Problems with bones can therefore be helped here, as well as teeth. Those with tinnitus, blurred vision and aching lower back can also be helped, or rather can help themselves. The Kidneys also govern water, including that which extracts the dirty from the clean, thereby making urinary problems a target for this meditation too. The kidneys also play a role in healthy breathing, as they are viewed as holding the energy from the lungs down. Breathing problems of any kind can benefit here. The kidneys and their energy are seen as manifesting in the hair, relying on them for nourishment to keep the hair glossy and healthy. If this is a problem, use this meditation.

Lastly the kidney house the will and control fear. As the kidneys are seen as the root of life, these basic functions are connected to the efficient working of the kidneys. If you suffer from fear, rational or unexplained, use this meditation. If you have a low will and lack of

207

motivation, this meditation can help. If you simply feel that you cannot face life and all its pressures this meditation can help you recover a degree of inner strength that is lacking, to help you.

The bladder is viewed in Chinese medicine as having the important function of governing the passing of urine. Any disharmony here can therefore be helped with this meditation. Signs to look for are infrequency in urine passing, pain when doing so and extreme amounts.

When you are ready to begin this meditation, begin in the usual manner with your grounding and connecting and become conscious of any specific problems you are treating. Become balanced and aware of the energy level of your system and then focus your concentration on the sphere of energy.

Focus it forming at a point on your right foot on the inner, underside of the sole. From here move the ball of energy slowly and steadily up and back to your ankle and then up through the back of your leg to the inner side of your knee. From here continue gently with the kidney meridian up through your leg and then straight on up through your body to a point on the right side of your chest just below the shoulder bone. This will be on a point just above the right side of your breast bone. Finish the movement of your energy sphere here and pause. Take stock and when you are ready repeat the path of the kidney meridian on the left side moving up the left leg and left side of your body.

Now focus on the path of the bladder meridian. This begins above the right eye in the centre and moves up and over the head in a straight line from here. Move your sphere of energy, smoothing out blockages as you go over the head and down the back, just a little to the right of the spine. Continue down in this straight line until you reach the base of the spine and back. Then move up about two inches and across the spine and then curve back down over the buttocks to a point on the top of your leg, in the centre at the back. From here simply drop down through your right leg and lastly move along the outer side of your right foot, finishing on the tip of the little toe. After this rather complicated path pause a little and become conscious of how you now feel.

When you are ready repeat the bladder meridian path beginning above your left eye, moving over the head and down the other side of the body and left leg, as before. Take a moment to become aware again of what you sense and realise now and when you are ready to, make your return by grounding yourself and returning to your meditation.

Heart Constrictor Meridian and Triple Heater Meridian Meditation

The Heart Constrictor meridian, also known as the Pericardium meridian, deals with the circulatory system of the body. Its function is closely related to that of the heart, the pericardium being the membrane that encloses the heart. The meditation for this energy channel helps to ensure the physical flow of blood around the body is fluid, smooth and even, so vital for many of the body's systems to function healthily. Since we are dealing with things at a meditational level, we may also find that thoughts may occur to us that illustrate our circulation through life – how we are allowing new things, thoughts, ideas, people, emotions etc. to come and go through us and our lives. Do be aware of this aspect as you perform this meditation.

The pericardium is seen as protecting the heart, so we can turn our attention to protecting our true selves as well as protecting from invasion by fever, infection and such like. If you have any kind of fever or infection, use this meditation.

The Triple Heater Meridian is sometimes called the triple warmer and is also known as the San Jiao, in Chinese medicine. The concept

209

of what San Jiao actually is, is another complex one, as there is no equivalent in Western medicine. The main function here is to coordinate water movements in the body, governing this function. The Triple Heater meridian also regulates the warming function of the body. As you perform this meditation, it is good to be aware of the temperature of your body, noticing any changes as you proceed. Those things which you feel heated about or are distinctly cool towards may also be highlighted during this technique.

Begin with your grounding and connecting in the usual way and then bring to mind that which you are treating, if anything specifically. Remember that this is not a prerequisite for the meridian meditation. Focus on the sphere of energy forming then at the beginning of the meridian and moving it along in the usual way, at a comfortable pace for you.

The heart constrictor meridian begins on the left side of your chest, at a point a little to the outside of the nipple. Remember that the path of the meridians is inside the body. From here, this meridian moves up and out, over the armpit to flow down the arm itself, down the inside of the centre. This energy vessel then moves through the hand until it reaches the end of the middle finger. When you have reached this point in your meditation, pause and take stock as before, bringing to a conscious level what you feel happened during the technique. Then repeat the path of the heart constrictor meridian down your left arm and hand.

When you are ready, focus then on the path of the triple heater meridian. This begins at the side of the left ear and moves back and around the ear over your head. From here move in your awareness down to the centre of the top of your back and then across your back to your left shoulder. Move down the arm in the centre at the back and right down to the hand. Move through the hand and out to the tip of the first finger. Pause again and repeat for the right side and then ground once more, completing this meditation in the usual way.

Liver Meridian and Gall Bladder Meridian Meditation

The liver has the function of storing blood, regulating the amount in circulation. This varies depending on activity and the specifics of each individual. When more blood is required the liver releases it, storing it until such a time occurs. Weakness and stiffness are signs that the liver function is impaired, so if you have these, use this meditation. The liver also has the vital function of ensuring the smooth flow of energy throughout the body, essential to the healthy functioning of the body.

The liver also controls the tendons and nails, ensuring that these function properly. The liver is regarded as opening into the eyes, so eye problems can be helped with this meditation. The liver is also viewed as enabling us to establish and keep control, not just of our bodies' functions, but of temperance in mind and spirit too. If you feel unbalanced, out of control or have a problem or deficiency in any of the above areas, do use this meditation to help yourself.

The gall bladder stores bile, a substance excreted into the digestive tract to aid the digestion process. If you cannot digest your food, or any aspect of your life, use this meditation. The gall bladder is also looked upon as dominating decision making, so if you have any problems here, this is an excellent meditation. Librans, like myself, are especially encouraged to use this meditation.

The path of the liver meridian begins on the big toe, first with the right foot. Move up through your foot and up through the inside of the centre of your leg to your pelvis. At this level, move out to the side of your body, level with the bottom of your ribs. Then move diagonally in and upwards for a distance of about two inches. When you have taken a moment to pause and rest, repeat this for the left leg and side of the body. Then move on the gall bladder meridian.

211

This begins at the outside of the right eye and moves straight back to the ear, moving up and around the ear and then straight down from behind the ear to the base of the neck at the side. From here curve down the side of your body to beneath the armpit. This meridian then zig-zags down across the ribs and to a point at the side of the top of the leg. From here we move down through the leg to the ankle, finally curving out to move through the side of the foot to the end of the second toe. When you have reached this point, pause and then repeat for the left side of the body. Remember to perform your grounding and connecting first and to be clear with your visualisation of the energy sphere, also grounding clearly afterwards.

Conception Vessel Meridian and Governing Vessel Meridian Meditation.

We come now to the last of the meridian energy vessel lines on which we shall meditate, called the Governing Vessel and Conception Vessel respectively. We can take the properties of these meridian lines from their names. The first, the conception vessel, deals with what we are conceiving in life. We can give thought to what is coming into our lives and ourselves, what is inspiring us, what is new, what we are just beginning to get a feel for, and what we wish to create at this time.

The Governing vessel does what you may imagine, in that it governs the overall function of the body and its systems. This meditation is a good one to use for an overall energy cleansing and if you have a general feeling of sickness or being unwell, but do not know the reason. General debilitating conditions such as M.E. or Seasonal Affective Disorder can also be helped by cleansing this meridian energy line. As such we can indeed govern our own choices of whether to be healthy or not.

The form of meditation is the same as before, beginning with the grounding and connecting, then visualising the movement of the sphere of energy along the meridian lines. Pause between the lines and then ground yourself when you have finished.

The path of Conception vessel begins at the centre of the body at the level of the base of your spine and the pubic bone, from the front. From here it simply moves up in a straight line until it reaches your lower lip, where it ends. This moves right through the centre of your body and as such links with the chakras we have dealt with before. As such it can give rise to some quite powerful sensations and energies, so do be gentle with yourself as you use this meditation.

Pause and when you are ready to continue, focus on a point above your top lip, again in the centre, where the Governing Vessel meridian begins. From here it moves again in a straight line over your head and down the centre of your back, again linking with the chakras, until it reaches the base of the spine, where it ends.

The technique for the meridian meditations is as follows:

Ground and connect
Become aware of what you are treating, if anything specific
Visualise energy sphere along the path of the meridian lines
Pause and take stock for realisation
Ground

We have now completed the series of seven meridian meditations, designed to return or maintain healthy functioning of the bodily systems. If you find difficulty in sensing the energy sphere moving along your meridians, it may be helpful to move your fingers along the path beforehand, gently massaging as you go. This will in itself stimulate a greater flow of energy as well as increasing your awareness of it. It is also very pleasurable!

It is but a short step from here to realising how these meditations can be combined with the energy system meditation in the last Chapter to provide and effective meditation system for the production and maintenance of Bod, Mind and Spirit. This system of healing meditation focuses on specific ailments and dis-eases of the functions of the body. We now turn our attention to other ways in which meditation can be used for healing.

BIBLIOGRAPHY

Peter Aziz – Shamanic Healing, Points Press, 1994

Barbara Ann Brennan – Hands of Light – Bantam, 1988

Barbara Ann Brennan – Light Emerging, Bantam, 1993

Ftitjof Capra – The Tao of Physics, Flamingo, 1976

John Davidson – Subtle Energy, C.W.Daniel, 1987

Marian Green – The Gentle Art of Aquarian Magic, 1987

Louise Hay – You Can Heal Your Life, Eden Grove Editions, 1984

Benjamin Hoff - The Tao of Pooh, Mandarin, 1982

Steve Hounsome – Taming The Wolf: Full Moon Meditations, Capall Bann, 1995

Pete Jennings & Pete Sawyer – Pathworking, Capall Bann, 1993

Jessica Macbeth – Moon Over Water, Gateway Books, 1990

Jessica Macbeth – Sun Over Mountain, Gateway Books, 1991 Louise Proto – Coming Alive, Thorsons, 1983

Serena Roney-Dougal – Where Science and Magic Meet, Element, 1991

Stuart Wilde – The Force, White Dove International, 1984

Stuart Wilde – The Quickening, White Dove International, 1988

Tom Williams – Chinese Medicine, Element, 1995

BIOGRAPHY

Steve Hounsome has been involved in this field for over thirty years and has completed a wide variety of studies and activities in this time.

Steve holds qualifications in the following subjects –

- *Progressive Healing*
- *Psychic Studies*
- *Esoteric Soul Healing*
- *Tarot*
- *Bach Flower Remedies*
- *Basic Counselling Skills*

The training Steve has completed is as follows –

- *One year Progressive Healing, Sanctuary of Progress*
- *One year Psychic Studies, Sanctuary of Progress*
- *Meditation - 2 years, private tutor*
- *Natural Magic, 1 year, Marian Green*
- *Ritual Magic, 1 year, The London Group*
- *Esoteric Soul Healing, 2 years, Isle of Avalon Foundation*
- *Bach Flower Remedies - Foundation Level Certificate*
- *Order of Bards, Ovates and Druids - 12 years, now initiated Druid member*

Steve has also attended lectures and workshops too numerous to mention over the years and continues to add to his knowledge and experience by attending events as they occur and maintaining his own regular sacred practices in Meditation, Yoga and Chi Kung. Steve has had articles published in many magazines, on a variety of the subjects he works in. These include Positive Health and Pagan Dawn, as well as many of the smaller titles produced in the Pagan and holistic communities.

Steve has appeared on TV, twice alongside Derek Acorah on Granada TV's show 'Psychic Livetime' and acted as examiner on the Living TV series 'Jane Goldman Investigates', overseeing the work of Michelle Knight who taught the Tarot to Jane.

Steve acted as advisor and consultant for the New World 'Music of the Tarot' CD, for which he also wrote the accompanying booklet.

Steve has had eight books published –

- *Taming the Wolf: Full Moon Meditations*
- *Practical Meditation*
- *Practical Spirituality*
- *Tarot Therapy Vol. 1: Tarot for the New Millenium*
- *Tarot Therapy Vol 2: Major Arcana, The Seekers Quest*
- *Tarot Therapy Vol. 3: Minor Arcana, The Map of the Quest*
- *How To Be A Telephone Psychic*
- *The Tarot Therapy Deck*

Steve has also produced his own unique card sets –

- *The Tarot Therapy Cards*
- *Chakra Affirmation Cards*
- *Tarot Therapy Affirmation Cards*

Steve has also produced a range of 15 highly-acclaimed Meditation and Development CD's, which you can see full details of in the Shop on this website.

Steve has taught in person across the South of England and by distance learning internationally. Apart from his own private events, Steve has taught at Adult Education Centres in Hampshire and was tutor of the 2-year Tarot course at the prestigious 'Isle of Avalon Foundation' in Glastonbury, Somerset. Steve has tested and trained psychic readers for some of the leading telephone psychic companies in the UK, working across the world.

Steve was a Founder Member and Secretary of the Professional Tarot Society and was also Secretary of the British Psychic Registration Board, although both these organisations are no longer in existence. Steve is now a member of the following organisations —

* Order of Bards, Ovates and Druids (Steve acts as mentor for those following their training programme)
* *Spiritual Workers Association*
* *Tarot Association of the British Isles*
* *British Astrologers and Psychics Society*
* *Tarot Professionals*

Though a member of these Groups, Steve's approach to spirituality is an eclectic one, as he feels that every path has something to offer. He reads widely on spiritual subjects and incorporates what he learns into his teaching, in its various forms. Steve feels that a sense of the sacred for each individual is vital to the maintenance of health and well-being and for the fulfilment of our potential, development and life purpose. More personally, Steve has a deep love of many forms of music, runs long-distance and cycles. He enjoys visiting sacred and natural sites, runs, plays tennis, attends his local gym regularly as well as watching football, remaining loyal to his origins by supporting his home-town team, Brighton & Hove Albion. He is the father of two children, Dakota and Amber.

TAROT THERAPY PRODUCTS

Steve Hounsome produces a range of products and services, which are detailed below –

THE TAROT THERAPY DECK
Steve has created his own Tarot deck, aimed at the therapeutic use of the cards in consultations and for personal and spiritual development.

TAROT THERAPY TRAINING
There are three courses available, for those wishing to train as a Tarot Therapist –

- **INTRODUCTION** – For the complete beginner
- **CERTIFICATE** – For those wanting to read professionally for others
- **DIPLOMA** - For those wanting to develop their existing knowledge and ability

TAROT THERAPY READINGS, PAST LIVES, MEDIUMSHIP
Steve is available for readings either in person in Dorset, England, by 'phone or by email.

PERSONAL, PSYCHIC & SPIRITUAL DEVELOPMENT
Steve has produced a range of meditations and exercises for personal, psychic and spiritual development. These are available as cd's or as downloads from the website.

MEDITATION, PSYCHIC DEVELOPMENT & TAROT STUDY GROUPS
Steve runs groups in all the above subjects, as well as holding a series of workshops throughout the year, in Dorset, England.

Full details of all the above are available at Steve's website –

www.tarottherapy.co.uk

You can also email Steve at –

steve@tarottherapy.co.uk

Printed in Great Britain
by Amazon

25917886R00126